MALCOLM X
ON
AFRO-AMERICAN
HISTORY

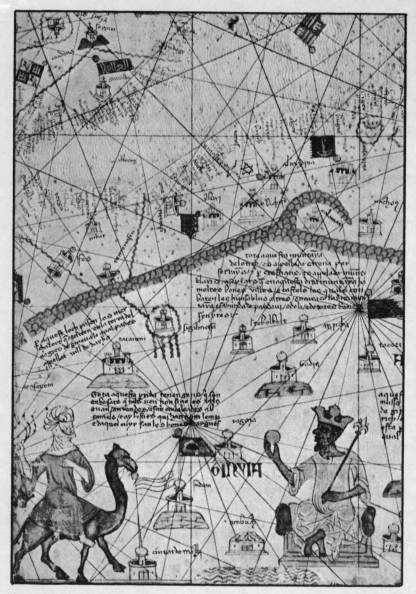

A map made in Catalonia (a province of Spain) in 1375 shows Mansa Musa, the Emperor of Mali. The mapmaker depicts "the richest king in Africa" holding up a gold nugget as an Arab trader approaches.

MALCOLM X ON AFRO-AMERICAN HISTORY

Expanded and Illustrated Edition

PATHFINDER

New York   London   Sydney   Toronto

Manufactured in the United States of America
Library of Congress Catalog Card Number 72-103696
ISBN 0-87348-085-6

First edition, 1967
Second edition, 1970
Ninth printing, 1988

Selections from The Autobiography of Malcolm X (copyright © 1964 by Alex Haley and Malcolm X; copyright © 1965 by Alex Haley and Betty Shabazz) are reprinted by permission of Grove Press, Inc.

Cover photo by Eli Finer

Pathfinder
410 West Street, New York, New York 10014
Distributors:
Africa, Europe, and the Middle East:
    Pathfinder, 47 The Cut, London, SE1 8LL, England
Asia, Australia, and the Pacific:
    Pathfinder, P.O. Box 153, Glebe, Sydney, NSW 2037,
        Australia
Canada:
    Pathfinder, 410 Adelaide St. W., Suite 400, Toronto,
        Ontario, M5V 1S8, Canada
New Zealand:
    Pilot Books, Box 8730, Auckland, New Zealand

CONTENTS

Bronze sculpture of warriors from Benin (Nigeria). Benin bronzes, dating back to fourteenth and fifteenth centuries, are world famous for the artistry and skill they incorporate.

INTRODUCTION

Malcolm X believed that the education, or re-education, of the black people of this country was necessary for the building of a new mass movement capable of fighting effectively for human rights. He therefore took every opportunity he could get — on television and radio, at press conferences, interviews and public meetings, large or small — to teach, to explain, to show the connections between various aspects of the freedom struggle, to induce people to think for themselves. He always adapted his speaking style to the particular audience he faced, using the vocabulary and the rhythm best suited for communication. The speech that follows, which has been transcribed from the tape of a public meeting on January 24, 1965, is typical of those he made in the last months of his life to the people of Harlem.

Malcolm left the Nation of Islam ("Black Muslims") in March, 1964, for reasons partly explained in this speech. That month he organized the Muslim Mosque, Inc., and in June, 1964, he founded the non-religious Organization of Afro-American Unity. He was abroad — in Africa, the Middle East and Europe — during half of this independent phase of his life, which ended after a short fifty weeks with his assassination in New York on February 21, 1965. Yet he managed, during the 25 weeks he spent at home, to hold 17 or 18 public rallies in Harlem, most of them at the Audubon Ballroom. It was in that hall, as he started to speak at one of those rallies, that he was killed.

Sometimes there were invited guest speakers at these public meetings — African students, Dick Gregory, Muhammad Babu of the Tanzanian cabinet, Fannie Lou Hamer; Che Guevara was invited once, but couldn't make it, and sent a message of solidarity. Sometimes films were shown. But the main speaker was usually Malcolm himself. He was often overworked and exhausted, but he was never too tired to present, patiently and calmly, facts and ideas and arguments that he believed his brothers and sisters needed to arm themselves for the freedom fight.

The January 24, 1965, speech was typical of his final period, but it also had special features. At that time the leaders of the Organization of Afro-American Unity had decided that their organization needed a new program. To arouse interest in it, they arranged a series of three public meetings at the Audubon. At the first of these (January 24), Malcolm was to speak on Afro-American history, from the ancient black civilizations through slavery to the present day. At the second (January 31), he was to discuss current conditions and the methods used to keep black people oppressed. At the third (which would have been February 7, although Malcolm twice made a mistake about that date in his January 24 talk), he was to speak about the future of the Afro-American struggle and the new OAAU program was to be presented.

This schedule was never completed. Malcolm did speak about the past on January 24, and he did speak about the present on January 31, but the third meeting was not held on February 7, because Malcolm had some important speaking engagements in England and France that week.

The third meeting in the Audubon series therefore was postponed to Monday, February 15; the regular Sunday time was not possible because Malcolm was scheduled to speak in Detroit on February 14. But a few hours after Malcolm's return from England, his home was fire-bombed, early in the morning of February 14, while he, his wife and four children were asleep. As a result, the February 15 meeting was devoted to a discussion of the bombing, and the presentation of the new OAAU program was postponed. At the next meeting, February 21, Malcolm was shot down as he started to speak at the Audubon.

Two other Audubon speeches (December 13 and December 20, 1964) will be found in the collection, *Malcolm X Speaks* (Merit Publishers, 1965, and Grove Press, 1966). The text of the OAAU program, which Malcolm approved although he did not write it, is printed as an appendix in my book, *The Last Year of Malcolm X: The Evolution of a Revolutionary* (Merit Publishers, 1967).

George Breitman

MALCOLM X ON
AFRO-AMERICAN HISTORY

Brothers and sisters: First I want to, as Brother James has pointed out, thank you, as we do each week, or have been doing each week. It seems that during the month of January it doesn't snow or rain or hail or get bad in any way weather-wise until Saturday night, and it stays like that Saturday through Sunday, and then the sun comes back out on Monday—it seems. But since I was a little boy I learned that one of the things that make you grow into manhood are tests and trials and tribulations. If you can come through the snow and the rain and the sleet, you know you can make it easily when the sun is out and everything is right. So I'm happy to see that those of you who are here tonight don't let anything get in your way, that is, weather-wise.

During the next three weeks, we're going to have a series that will be designed to give us a better understanding of the past, I should say a better knowledge of the past, in order that we may understand the present and be better prepared for the future. I don't think any of you will deny the fact that it is impossible to understand the present or prepare for the future unless we have some knowledge of the past. And the thing that has kept most of us, that is, the Afro-Americans, almost crippled in this society has been our complete lack of knowledge concerning the past. The number one thing that makes us differ from other people is our lack of knowledge concerning the past. Proof of which—almost anyone else can come into this country and get around barriers and obstacles that we cannot get around; and the only difference between them and us, they know something about the past, and in knowing something about the past, they know something about themselves, they have an identity. But wherein

3

you and I differ from them is primarily revolved around our lack of knowledge concerning the past. And tonight, this is what we would like to go into. Next Sunday night, it's our intention to go into the present, some of the tricks that are used to keep us at the level that we are on by making us think that we're going forward when we are actually standing still. And then the third Sunday night, the 31st, it's the intention of the Organization of Afro-American Unity at that time to spell out what we think are the best steps to take, and at that time also offer a program that we feel Harlem, people in Harlem, can participate in toward getting that objective or solution into becoming a reality.

When you deal with the past, you're dealing with history, you're dealing actually with the origin of a thing. When you know the origin, you know the cause. If you don't know the origin, you don't know the cause. And if you don't know the cause, you don't know the reason, you're just cut off, you're left standing in mid-air. So the past deals with history or the origin of anything — the origin of a person, the origin of a nation, the origin of an incident. And when you know the origin, then you get a better understanding of the causes that produce whatever originated there and its reason for originating and its reason for being. It's impossible for you and me to have a balanced mind in this society without going into the past, because in this particular society, as we function and fit into it right now, we're such an underdog, we're trampled upon, we're looked upon as almost nothing. Now if we don't go into the past and find out how we got this way, we will think that we were always this way. And if you think that you were always in the condition that you're in right now, it's impossible for you to have too much confidence in yourself, you become worthless, almost nothing. But when you go back into the past and find out where you once were, then you will know that you weren't always at this level, that you once had attained a higher level, had made great achievements, contributions to society, civilization, science and so forth. And you know that if you once did it, you can do it again; you automatically get the incentive, the inspiration and the energy necessary to duplicate what our forefathers formerly did. But by keeping us completely cut off from our past, it is easy for the man who has power over us to make us willing to stay at this level because we will feel that we

4

were always at this level, a low level. That's why I say it is so important for you and me to spend time today learning something about the past so that we can better understand the present, analyze it, and then do something about it.

The Internationalist Viewpoint

One of the main things that you will find when you compare people who come out here on Sunday nights with other people is that those who come here have interests that go beyond local interests or even national interests. I think you will find most who come out here are interested in things local, and interested in things national, but are also interested in things international. Most Afro-Americans who go to other meetings are usually interested in things local — Harlem, that's it; or Mississippi, that's it — national. But seldom do you find them taking a keen interest in things going on world-wide, because they don't know what part they play in things going on world-wide. But those of us who come here, come here because we not only see the importance of having an understanding of things local and things national, but we see today the importance of having an understanding of things international, and where our people, the Afro-Americans in this country, fit into that scheme of things, where things international are concerned. We come out because our scope is broad, our scope is international rather than national, and our interests are international, rather than national. Our interests are world-wide, rather than limited just to things American, or things New York, or things Mississippi. And this is very important. You can get into a conversation with a person, and in five minutes tell whether or not that person's scope is broad or whether that person's scope is narrow, whether that person is interested in things going on in his block where he lives or interested in things going on all over the world. Now persons who are narrow-minded, because their knowledge is limited, think that they're affected only by things happening in their block. But when you find a person who has a knowledge of things of the world today, he realizes that what happens in South Vietnam can affect him if he's living on St. Nicholas Avenue, or what's happening in the Congo affected his situation on 8th Avenue or 7th Avenue

5

or Lenox Avenue. The person who realizes the effect that things all over the world have right on his block, on his salary, on his reception or lack of reception into society, immediately becomes interested in things international. But if a person's scope is so limited that he thinks things that affect him are only those things that take place across the street or downtown, then he's only interested in things across the street and downtown. So, one of our greatest desires here at Organization of Afro-American Unity meetings is to try and broaden the scope and even the reading habits of most of our people, who need their scope broadened and their reading habits also broadened today.

Another thing that you will find is that those who go to other places usually think of themselves as a minority. If you'll notice, in all of their struggling, programming or even crying or demanding, they even refer to themselves as a minority, and they use a minority approach. By a minority they mean that they are lesser than something else, or they are outnumbered, or the odds are against them — and this is the approach that they use in their argument, in their demand, in their negotiation. But when you find those of us who have been following the nationalistic thinking that prevails in Harlem, we don't think of ourselves as a minority, because we don't think of ourselves just within the context of the American stage or the American scene, in which we would be a minority. We think of things worldly, or as the world is; we think of our part in the world, and we look upon ourselves not as a dark minority on the white American stage, but rather we look upon ourselves as a part of the dark majority who now prevail on the world stage. And when you think like this automatically, when you realize you are part of the majority, you approach your problem as if odds are on your side rather than odds are against you. You approach demanding rather than using the begging approach. And this is one of the things that is frightening the white man. As long as the black man in America thinks of himself as a minority, as an underdog, he can't shout but so loud; or if he does shout, he shouts loudly only to the degree that the power structure encourages him to. He never gets irresponsible. He never goes beyond what the power structure thinks is the right voice to shout in. But when you begin to connect yourself on the world stage with the whole of dark mankind, and you see that you're the majority and this majority is waking up and rising up and becoming strong, then when you deal with this man, you don't deal with him like he's your boss or he's better than you or stronger than you. You put him right where he belongs. When you realize that he's a minority, that his time is running out, you approach him like that, you approach him like one who used to be strong but is now getting weak, who used to be in a position to retaliate against you but now is not in that position anymore.

When you jump out around some black Americans and speak as if everything is on your side, why, they think you're crazy. But they think you're crazy because they can't see what you see. All they see is Charlie, all they see is the white man. And because he is all they see, to them he looks like a giant. But you're looking beyond the white man. You see the nations of the earth that are black, brown, red and yellow, who used to be down, now getting up. And when you see them, you find that you look more like them than you look like Sam. And then you find yourself relating to them, whereas you formerly tried to relate to Sam. When you relate to them, you're related to the majority. But when you relate to Uncle Sam, you automatically become a minority relative. You understand?

He examines us all the time. He has the black community throughout this land always under a microscope just like in a scientist's laboratory, to find out how you're thinking, to keep up to date on how you think, on the beat of your pulse — are you beating too hot, or is your temperature running too hot, or is it cool? He wants to know how you think and how you feel. If you seem to be working up a temperature that he's not responsible for, it worries him. As long as your temperature rises when he puts the pressure, that's okay. But if he sees you making some reactions that are motivated other than by something that he has done, then he begins to worry. He finds that something else is influencing you and controlling you beyond his control and influence. And he should worry when you begin to get like that.

Whether you come to the meetings of the Organization of Afro-American Unity or not, whether you go to church today or into the lodge or anywhere, there is one thing that everyone agrees — that the world is in trouble. Whether you go to church, the mosque, the synagogue, or are just a plain atheist and go to the pool room, or someplace else, there's one thing that everyone has to agree upon, and that is that the world is in trouble, the world is in real trouble. There are many different spots in the world today that could cause it to explode. And it's in multiple trouble since China exploded the atomic bomb. Formerly, when just the white nations had it, they went according to certain rules, rules laid down by them. They've always done this. They lay down rules but the rules are always in their favor. But they have already learned through history that the dark nation that becomes truly independent intellectually doesn't necessarily go by their rules. The Japanese proved this when they hit Pearl Harbor. They'd smile and *bop* — let you have it. Well, this is true, this goes beyond the ground rules that they laid down and it gets unexpected results. The Japanese proved their ability to do this with Pearl Harbor, which is intelligent in my opinion — I don't think that anybody should tell somebody else what they're going to do; they should go ahead and do it, and that's it. Because you might say what you're going to do, and not get a chance to do it, and you look bad; not only do you feel bad, you end up looking bad. So it's better to go ahead and do it. I think they had the right philosophy there myself. And the Chinese can do it even better than that. They've got more people to do it with, and now they've got more explosiveness to do it with.

A New Balance of Power

So we're living in troubled times. We're living at a time when anything can happen. Just a couple of years ago it couldn't happen unless Sam said so, or unless Khrushchev said so, or unless de Gaulle said so. But now it can happen any time. It's not in the power of just one race to say when this can happen or when that can happen; it can now be set off by dark nations. So the world is in trouble. Another characteristic of this era that we're living in, that's causing it to be a troubled world, is the fact that the dark world is rising. And as the dark world rises, the white world declines. It's impossible for the dark world to increase in its power and strength without the power and strength of the white world decreasing.

8

This is just the way it is, it's almost mathematics. If there is only so much power, and all of it has been over there, well, the only way this man's going to get some over here is to take it away from those over there. That's plain fact. Up until recent times, all of the power has been in Europe, it has all been in the hands of the white man. The base of power has been in London and Paris and Brussels and Washington, D. C., and some of those places like that. Now the bases of power are changing. You have a base of power in Accra, in Ghana, in Africa. Another base of power in Zanzibar. Another base of power in Cairo. Another base of power in Algiers. Another base of power in Tokyo. Another base of power in Peking. Well, as these bases of power increase, it decreases Europe as a base of power. And this is what's causing trouble. The white man is worried. He knows that he didn't do right when he had all the power, and if the base of power changes, those into whose hands it falls may know how to really do right. The rise of the dark world is producing the fall of the white world.

And I've got to point out right here that what I'm saying is not racist; I'm not speaking racism, I'm not condemning all white people. I'm just saying that in the past the white world was in power, and it was. This is history, this is fact. They called it European history, or colonialism. They ruled all the dark world. Now when they were in power and had everything going their way, they didn't call that racism, they called it colonialism. And they were happy too when they could stand up and tell how much power they had. Britain used to brag about the sun never set on her empire. Her empire was so vast, you know, that the sun would never set on it, she bragged. I heard Churchill say it, and Macmillan, and some of those others who sat over there telling everybody else what to do. But now the shoe is on the other foot. There is no nation today that can brag about its power being unlimited, or that it can take unilateral action in any area of the earth that they desire. No white nation can do this. But just 20 years ago they could do it. Twenty years ago the United States could do it, 20 years ago England could do it, France could do it, even little old runt Belgium could do it, and Holland could do it. But they can't do it now. Because the base of power is shifting. And this is what you and I have to understand, really, in order to understand what's happening in

Georgia, in Alabama, in Mississippi and in New York City.

The power is shifting, and as it shifts, the man in whose hands it once was gets worried, and the man in whose hands it falls, who hasn't had it for a long time, he gets power-happy, you know, and he is not particularly interested in playing according to the rules, especially the rules that this man laid down. Now as the base of power shifts, what it is doing is bringing an end to what you and I know to have been white supremacy. Supreme means to be above others. And up until recent times, the white nations were above the dark nations. They ruled supreme on this earth. They didn't call it white supremacy, but this is what it was. Now white supremacy has come to an end. Only meaning that the time when the white man could reign supreme all over the world — that's ended, that's outdated, that's gone by, it can't happen any more. And it is reflected in what Macmillan meant when he spoke in Africa three years ago about the winds of change. At this time Macmillan was the prime minister of England and he was making a tour through Africa; and he came back crying to the other Europeans about the winds of change that are sweeping down across the African continent, meaning that the people who formerly had permitted Europeans or whites to oppress them had changed their minds. They didn't want to be oppressed any longer, they didn't want to be exploited any longer, they wanted to be independent and free to build a society of their own for themselves.

As soon as this mood or tempo began to be visible on the African continent, some of this earth's leading white statesmen at the top level admitted it — and didn't admit it secretly, admitted it openly. Adlai Stevenson got up in the United Nations, I think it was last year, and accused the dark nations of playing a skin game in the UN. And you know what he meant by skin game? He meant that people of the same skin color were banding together. Meaning that people with dark skins were banding together in the UN against people with white skins. This is something to think about. Now this means that the United States representative to the United Nations, an international body, was alert enough, had sufficient foresight, to see that in this era that we're living in right now, dark-skinned people were coming together, they were uniting, they were forming blocs — the Afro-Asian bloc, the Afro-Asian-Arab bloc, the Afro-Asian-Arab-Latin bloc, you know—and all these blocs were against him. He could see this, and this is what caused so much worry and so much confusion today.

As soon as he saw that these dark-skinned people were getting together in unity and harmony, he began to put out the propaganda that the dark-skinned people aren't ready yet. This is his analysis after our efforts—that we aren't ready for freedom. And to try and prove that we weren't ready for freedom, they let the people in the Congo go so far free and then turned right around and stirred it up to make them look foolish—so that they could use that to say that Africa wasn't ready for freedom. They say the same thing to you and me over here, that we're not ready yet—isn't that what they say? Certainly, they say that you're not ready to live in a decent house, and that you're not ready to go to a decent school, or that you're not ready to work on a decent job. This is what they say, and they don't say why we're not ready, they don't say why. And if we're not ready, they don't say that we once were ready, but we're not now—they try and make it look like we never were ready, that we never were in history a people who occupied a responsible position on the cultural tree, the civilization tree, or any other tree. They try to give us the impression, you know, that we never were qualified, therefore we can only qualify today to the degree that they themselves qualify us. And they trick us this way. Trick us into going to them and asking them, "Qualify me, you know, so I can be free." Why, you're out of your mind.

The Trap of "Racism"

They also know that the only way we're going to do it is through unity. So they create another trap. Every effort we make to unite among ourselves on the basis of what we are, they label it as what?—racism. If we say that we want to form something that's based on black people getting together, the white man calls that racism. Mind you, this is right. And then some of these old white-minded Negroes do the same thing, they say, "That's racism, I don't want to belong to anything that's all-black." A lot of them say this. But it's only because they themselves have been bitten by the bug, the white bug. And they think the only way they can belong to something

11

that is going to be progressive or successful, it has got to have the white man in it. Many of them think that. But these are traps. He traps us because he knows it's impossible for us to go forward unless we get together. But what basis are we going to get together on? We've got to get together on the same basis they got together. Italians got together because they were Italian, the Jews got together on the basis of being Jews, the Irish got together on the basis of being Irish. Now what basis are you and I going to get together on? We've got to have some kind of basis. But as soon as we mention the only basis that we've got to get together on, they trick us by telling our leaders, you know, that anything that's all-black is putting segregation in reverse. Isn't that what they say? So the people who are black don't want to get together because they don't want segregation — see, the man is tricky, brothers and sisters. I mean the man is tricky. He's a master of tricks. And if you don't realize how tricky he is, he'll have you maneuvered right back into slavery. I shouldn't say back into slavery because we're not out of it yet.

These are traps that he creates. If you speak in an angry way about what has happened to our people and what is happening to our people, what does he call it? Emotionalism. Pick up on that. Here the man has got a rope around his neck and because he screams, you know, the cracker that's putting the rope around his neck accuses him of being emotional. You're supposed to have the rope around your neck and holler politely, you know. You're supposed to watch your diction, not shout and wake other people up — this is how you're supposed to holler. You're supposed to be respectable and responsible when you holler against what they're doing to you. And you've got a lot of Afro-Americans who fall for that. They say, "No, you can't do it like that, you've got to be responsible, you've got to be respectable." And you'll always be a slave as long as you're trying to be responsible and respectable in the eyesight of your master; you'll remain a slave. When you're in the eyesight of your master, you've got to let him know you're irresponsible and you'll blow his irresponsible head off.

And again you've got another trap that he maneuvers you into. If you begin to talk about what he did to you, he'll say that's hate, you're teaching hate. Pick up on that. He won't say he didn't do it, because he can't. But he'll accuse you of

12

teaching hate just because you begin to spell out what he did to you. Which is an intellectual trap — because he knows we don't want to be accused of hate. And the average black American who has been real brainwashed, he never wants to be accused of being emotional. You ever watched them? You ever watched one of them? Do that — watch them, watch the real bourgeois black Americans. He never wants to show any sign of emotion. He won't even tap his feet. You can have some of that real soul music, and he'll sit there, you know, like it doesn't move him. I watch him, and I'm telling you. And the reason he tries to pretend like it doesn't move him is that he knows it doesn't move them. And it doesn't move them because they can't feel it, they've got no soul. And he's got to pretend he has none just to make it with them. This is a shame, really.

And then you go a step farther, they get you again on this violence. They have another trap wherein they make it look criminal if any of us, who has a rope around his neck or one is being put around his neck — if you do anything to stop the man from putting that rope around your neck, that's violence. And again this bourgeois Negro, who's trying to be polite and respectable and all, he never wants to be identified with violence. So he lets them do anything to him, and he sits there submitting to it non-violently, just so he can keep his image of responsibility. He dies with a responsible image, he dies with a polite image, but he dies. The man who is irresponsible and impolite, he keeps his life. That responsible Negro, he'll die every day, but the irresponsible one dies and takes some of those with him who were trying to make him die.

So the era that we're living in is an era in which we see the people in the East on the rise and the people in the West on the decline. That is, the dark world is rising and the white world or the Western world is having its power curtailed. This is happening and it's happening every day. Take right there is Saigon in South Vietnam. Don't you realize that 20 years ago those little people over there didn't have a chance? All they needed would be for a battleship to sail up to the coast-line, and everybody over there would bow down, "Yessir, boss." That's how they said it, same as you say it over here. But not now. Now they don't yes anybody's boss. They get them a rifle and run boss clean on out of there. The entire

13

East, the dark world, is on the rise. Whether you like it or not. And as the dark world rises up, it puts the white world on the spot, it puts the Western world on the spot, and it puts you and me on the spot. Why does it put us on the spot? Because although we're in the *West*, we're from the *East*. Many, many black Americans don't realize this. You are not *of* the West, you are *in* the West. You're not a Westerner, you're from the East. You're not white — you're in the white world, but that doesn't make you white; you're as black as you ever were, you're just in the white world.

Negro History Week

And next month they'll come up to show you another trick. They'll come at you and me next month with this Negro History Week, they call it. This week comes around once every year. And during this one week they drown us with propaganda about Negro history in Georgia and Mississippi and Alabama. Never do they take us back across the water, back home. They take us down home, but they never give us a history of back home. They never give us enough information to let us know what were we doing before we ended up in Mississippi, Alabama, Georgia, Texas, and some of those other prison states. They give us the impression with Negro History Week that we were cotton pickers all of our lives. Cotton pickers, orange growers, mammies and uncles for the white man in this country — this is our history when you talk in terms of Negro History Week. They might tell you about one or two people who took a peanut and made another white man rich. George Washington Carver — he was a scientist, but he died broke. He made Ford rich. So he wasn't doing anything for himself and his people. He got a good name for us, but what did we get out of it? — nothing; the master got it.

Just like a dog who runs out of the woods and grabs a rabbit. No matter how hungry the dog is, does he eat it? No, he takes it back and lays it at the boss's feet. The boss skins it, takes the meat, and gives the dog the bones. And the dog is going right on, hungry again. But he could have gotten the rabbit and eaten it for himself. And boss couldn't even have caught him until later, because he can outrun the boss.

It's the same way with you and me. Every contribution we make, we don't make it for our people, we make it for the man, we make it for our master. He gets the benefit from it. We die, not for our people, we die for him. We don't die for our home and our house, we die for his house. We don't die for our country, we die for his country. A lot of you all were fools on the front lines, were you not? Yes, you were. You put on the uniform and went right up on the front lines like a roaring hound dog barking for master. And when you come back here—you've had to bark since you came back.

So Negro History Week reminds us of this. It doesn't remind us of past achievements, it reminds us only of the achievements we made in the Western hemisphere under the tutelage of the white man. So that whatever achievement that was made in the Western hemisphere that the spotlight is put upon, this is the white man's shrewd way of taking credit for whatever we have accomplished. But he never lets us know of an accomplishment that we made prior to being born here. This is another trick.

The worst trick of all is when he names us Negro and calls us Negro. And when we call ourselves that, we end up tricking ourselves. My brother Cassius was on the screen the other night talking with Les Crane about the word Negro. I wish he wouldn't have gone so fast, because he was in a position to have done a very good job. But he was right in saying that we're not Negroes, and have never been, until we were brought here and made into that. We were scientifically produced by the white man. Whenever you see somebody who calls himself a Negro, he's a product of Western civilization— not only Western civilization, but Western crime. The Negro, as he is called or calls himself in the West, is the best evidence that can be used against Western civilization today. One of the main reasons we are called Negro is so we won't know who we really are. And when you call yourself that, you don't know who you really are. You don't know what you are, you don't know where you came from, you don't know what is yours. As long as you call yourself a Negro, nothing is yours. No languages—you can't lay claim to any language, not even English; you mess it up. You can't lay claim to any name, any type of name, that will identify you as something that you should be. You can't lay claim to any culture as long as you use the word Negro to identify yourself. It attaches you to nothing. It doesn't even identify your color.

If you talk about one of them, they call themselves white, don't they? Or they might call someone else Puerto Rican to identify them. Mind you how they do this. When they call him a Puerto Rican, they're giving him a better name. Because there is a place called Puerto Rico, you know. It at least lets you know where he came from. So they'll say whites, Puerto Ricans and Negroes. Pick up on that. That's a drag, brothers. White is legitimate. It means that's what color they are. Puerto Rican tells you that they're someone else, came from somewhere else, but they're here now. Negro doesn't tell you anything. I mean nothing, absolutely nothing. What do you identify it with? — tell me — nothing. What do you attach it to, what do you attach to it? — nothing. It's completely in the middle of nowhere. And when you call yourself that, that's where you are — right in the middle of nowhere. It doesn't give you a language, because there is no such thing as a Negro language. It doesn't give you a country, because there is no such thing as a Negro country. It doesn't give you a culture — there is no such thing as a Negro culture, it doesn't exist. The land doesn't exist, the culture doesn't exist, the language doesn't exist, and the man doesn't exist. They take you out of existence by calling you a Negro. And you can walk around in front of them all day long and they act like they don't even see you. Because you made yourself nonexistent. It's a person who has no history; and by having no history, he has no culture.

Just as a tree without roots is dead, a people without history or cultural roots also becomes a dead people. And when you look at us, those of us who are called Negro, we're called that because we are like a dead people. We have nothing to identify ourselves as part of the human family. You know, you take a tree, you can tell what kind of tree it is by looking at the leaves. If the leaves are gone, you can look at the bark and tell what kind it is. But when you find a tree with the leaves gone and the bark gone, everything gone, you call that a what? — a stump; and you can't identify a stump as easily as you can identify a tree. And this is the position that you and I are in here in America. Formerly we could be identified by the names we wore when we came here. When we were first brought here, we had different names. When

16

we were first brought here, we had a different language. And these names and this language identified the culture that we were brought from, the land that we were brought from. In identifying that, we were able to point towards what we had produced, our net worth. But once our names were taken and our language was taken and our identity was destroyed and our roots were cut off with no history, we became like a stump, something dead, a twig over here in the Western hemisphere. Anybody could step on us, trample upon us or burn us, and there would be nothing that we could do about it.

Those of you who are religious, who go to church, [know] there are stories in the Bible that can be used easily to pretty well tell the condition of the black man in America once he became a Negro. They refer to him in there as the lost sheep, meaning someone who is lost from his own kind, which is how you and I have been for the past 400 years. We have been in a land where we are not citizens, or in a land where they have treated us as strangers. They have another symbolic story in there, called the dry bones. Many of you have gone to church Sunday after Sunday and got, you know, the ghost, they call it, got happy. When the old preacher started singing about dry bones, you'd knock over benches, just because he was singing about those bones, "them dry bones," (I know how they say it). But you never could identify the symbolic meaning of those bones — how they were dead because they had been cut off from their own kind. Our people here in America have been in the same condition as those dry bones that you sit in church singing about. But you shed more tears over those dry bones than you shed over yourself. This is a strange thing, but it shows what happens to a people when they are cut off and stripped of everything, like you and I have been cut off and stripped of everything. We become a people like no other people, and we are a people like no other people, [there's] no other people on earth like you and me. We're unique, we're different. They say that we're Negro, and they say that Negro means black; yet they don't call all black people Negroes. You see the contradiction? Mind you, they say that we're Negro, because Negro means black in Spanish, yet they don't call all black people Negroes. Something there doesn't add up.

And then to get around it they say mankind is divided up into three categories — Mongoloid, Caucasoid, and Negroid.

Now pick up on that. And all black people aren't Negroid—they've got some jet black ones that they classify as Caucasoid. But if you'll study very closely, all of the black ones that they classify as Caucasoid are those that still have great civilizations, or still have the remains of what was once a great civilization. The only ones that they classify as Negroid are those that they find with no evidence that they were ever civilized; then they call them Negroid. But they can't afford to let any black-skinned people who have evidence that they formerly occupied a high seat in civilization, they can't afford to let them be called Negroid, so they take them on into the Caucasoid classification.

And actually Caucasoid, Mongoloid and Negroid—there's no such thing. These are so-called anthropological terms that were put together by anthropologists who were nothing but agents of the colonial powers, and they were purposely given that status, they were purposely given such scientific positions, in order that they could come up with definitions that would justify the European domination over the Africans and the Asians. So immediately they invented classifications that would automatically demote these people or put them on a lesser level. All of the Caucasoids are on a high level, the Negroids are kept at a low level. This is just plain trickery that their scientists engage in in order to keep you and me thinking that we never were anything, and therefore he's doing us a favor as he lets us step upward or forward in his particular society or civilization. I hope you understand what I am saying.

Ancient Black Civilizations

Now then, once you see that the condition that we're in is directly related to our lack of knowledge concerning the history of the black man, only then can you realize the importance of knowing something about the history of the black man. The black man's history—when you refer to him as the black man you go way back, but when you refer to him as a Negro, you can only go as far back as the Negro goes. And when you go beyond the shores of America you can't find a Negro. So if you go beyond the shores of America in history, looking for the history of the black man, and you're looking for him under the term Negro, you won't find him. He doesn't exist. So you end up thinking that you didn't play any role in history.

But if you want to take the time to do research for yourself, I think you'll find that on the African continent there was always, prior to the discovery of America, there was always a higher level of history, rather a higher level of culture and civilization, than that which existed in Europe at the same time. At least 5,000 years ago they had a black civilization in the Middle East called the Sumerians. Now when they show you pictures of the Sumerians they try and make you think that they were white people. But if you go and read some of the ancient manuscripts or even read between the lines of some of the current writers, you'll find that the Sumerian civilization was a very dark-skinned civilization, and it existed prior even to the existence of the Babylonian empire, right in the same area where you find Iraq and the Tigris-Euphrates Rivers there. It was a black-skinned people who lived there, who had a high state of culture way back then.

And at a time even beyond this there was a black-skinned people in India, who were black, just as black as you and I, called Dravidians. They inhabited the sub-continent of India even before the present people that you see living there today, and they had a high state of culture. The present people of India even looked upon them as gods; most of their statues, if you'll notice, have pronounced African features. You go right to India today—in their religion, which is called Buddhism, they give all their Buddhas the image of a black man, with his lips and his nose, and even show his hair all curled up on his head; they didn't curl it up, he was born that way. And these people lived in that area before the present people of India lived there. The black man lived in the Middle East before the present people who are now living there. And he had a high culture and a high civilization, to say nothing about the oldest civilization of all that he had in Egypt along the banks of the Nile. And in Carthage in northwest Africa, another part of the continent, and at a later date in Mali and Ghana and Songhai and Moorish civilization—all of these civilizations existed on the African continent before America was discovered.

19

Now the black civilization that shook the white man up the most was the Egyptian civilization, and it was a black civilization. It was along the banks of the Nile which runs through the heart of Africa. But again this tricky white man, and he's tricky—and mind you again, when I say this, it's not a racist statement. Some of them might not be tricky, but all of them I've met are tricky. And his civilization shows his trickiness. This tricky white man was able to take the Egyptian civilization, write books about it, put pictures in those books, make movies for television and the theatre—so skillfully that he has even convinced other white people that the ancient Egyptians were white people themselves. They were African, they were as much African as you and I. And he even gave the clue away when he made this movie, "King Solomon's Mines," and he showed the Watusis, you know, with their black selves, and he outright admitted in there that they looked like the ancient pharaohs of ancient Egypt. Which means that the white man himself, he knows that the black man had this high civilization in Egypt, whose remains today show the black man in that area had mastered mathematics, had mastered architecture, the science of building things, had even mastered astronomy.

The pyramid, as the white scientists admit, is constructed in such a position on this earth to show that the black people who were the architects of it had a knowledge of geography that was so vast, they knew the exact center of the earth's land mass. Because the base of the pyramid is located in the exact center of the earth's land mass, which could not have been so situated by its architect unless the architect in that day had known that the earth was round and knew how much land there was in all the directions from where he was standing. The pyramid was built so many thousand years ago that they don't even know the exact time it was built, but they do know that the people who brought it into existence had mastered the science of building, had mastered the various sciences of the earth and had mastered astronomy. I read where one scientist said that the architect of the pyramid had built a shaft that went outward from the center of the pyramid, and the place it marked in the sky was the location where a star, a blue star I think, some kind of a star, made an appearance only once every 50,000 years. Now they say that this architect's knowledge of astronomy was so vast that he evidently had access to histories or records that spotlighted the existence of a star that made its appearance at a certain spot in the sky only once every 50,000 years. Now he could not have known this unless he had records going back beyond 50,000 years. Yet the pyramid is a living witness today that the black people who were responsible for bringing it into existence had this kind of knowledge.

When you read the opinions of the white scientists about the pyramids and the building of the pyramids, they don't make any secret at all over the fact that they marvel over the scientific ability that was in the possession of those people way back then. They had mastered chemistry to such extent that they could make paints whose color doesn't fade right until today. When I was in Cairo in the summer, I was in King Tut's tomb, plus, I saw that which was taken out of the tomb at the Cairo Museum, and the colors of the clothing that was worn and the colors inside the tomb are as bright and vivid and sharp today as they were when they were put there some thousands of years ago. Whereas, you know yourself, you can paint your house, and have to paint it again next year. This man hasn't learned how to make paint yet that will last two years. And the black man in that day was such a master in these various scientific fields that he left behind evidence that his scientific findings in that day exceeded the degree to which the white man here in the West has been able to rise today. And you must know this, because if you don't know this, you won't really understand what there is about you that makes them so afraid of you, and makes them show that they find it imperative for them to keep you down, keep you from getting up, because if they let you up one inch, you've got it and gone—just one inch, you've got it and gone. And you should get it and go.

Just behind the pyramids is a huge statue which many of you are familiar with, called the Sphinx. The people who live over there call it Abou Al-hole, which means "father of everything." This too was put over there so long ago they don't know who did it, nor do they know how long ago it was done. And they marvel at it. What causes them to marvel is the fact that the black man could have been at such a high level then, and now be where he is today, at the bottom of the heap, with no outer sign that he has any scientific ability left within him. And he himself doesn't believe that he has any of this ability within him; he thinks that he has to turn to the man for some kind of formula on even how to get his freedom or how to build his house. But the black man by nature is a builder, he is scientific by nature, he's mathematical by nature. Rhythm is mathematics, harmony is mathematics. It's balance. And the black man is balanced. Before you and I came over here, we were so well balanced we could toss something on our head and run with it. You can't even run with your hat now — you can't keep it on. Because you lost your balance. You've gotten away from yourself. But when you are in tune with yourself, your very nature has harmony, has rhythm, has mathematics. You can build. You don't even need anybody to teach you how to build. You play music by ear. You dance by how you're feeling. And you used to build the same way. You have it in you to do it. I know black brickmasons from the South who have never been to school a day in their life. They throw more bricks together and you don't know how they learned how to do it, but they know how to do it. When you see one of those other people doing it, they've been to school — somebody had to teach them. But nobody teaches you always what you know how to do. It just comes to you. That's what makes you dangerous. When you come to yourself, a whole lot of other things will start coming to you, and the man knows it.

European "Civilization"

In that day the black man in Egypt was wearing silk, sharp as a tack, brothers. And those people up in Europe didn't know what cloth was. They admit this. They were naked or they were wearing skins from animals. If they could get an animal, they would take his hide and throw it around their shoulders to keep warm. But they didn't know how to sew and weave. They didn't have that knowledge in Europe, not in those days. They didn't cook their food in Europe. Even they themselves will show you when they were living up there in caves, they were knocking animals in the head and eating the raw meat. They were eating raw meat, raw food. They still like it raw today. You watch them go in a restaurant, they say, "Give me a steak rare, with the blood dripping in it." And then you run in and say, "Give me one rare, with the blood dripping in it." You don't do it because that's the way you like it; you're just imitating them, you're copying, you're trying to be like that man. But when you act like yourself, you say, "Make mine well done." You like cooked food, because you've been cooking a long time; but they haven't been cooking so long — it wasn't too long ago that they knew what fire was. This is true.

You were walking erect, upright. You ever watch your walk? Now you do this to walk erect. You've come up with that other walk. But when you're yourself, you walk with dignity. Wherever you see the black man, he walks with dignity. They have a tendency to be other than with dignity, unless they're trained. When their little girls go up to these, you know, hifalutin' schools, and they want to teach them how to walk, they put a book on their head. Isn't that what they do? They teach them how to walk like you. That's what they're learning how to walk like, like you. But you were almost born with a book on your head. You can throw it up there and run with it. I was amazed when I was in Africa to see the sense of poise and balance that these people over there have, all throughout Africa and Asia. They have that poise and that balance. But this is not an accident. This comes from something. And you have it too, but you've been channeling yours in another direction, in a different direction. But when you come to yourself, you'll channel it right.

Also as I said earlier, at that same time there was another African civilization called Carthage. One of the most famous persons in Carthage was a man named Hannibal. You and I have been taught that he was a white man. This is how they steal your history, they steal your culture, they steal your civilization — just by Hollywood producing a movie showing a black man as a white man. I remember one day I told someone that Hannibal was black — some Negro, he was in college, you understand — I told him Hannibal was a black man, and he had a fit. Really, he did, he wanted to fight me

23

on that. He said, "I know better than that." "How do you know?" He said, "I saw him." "Where'd you see him?" He said, "In the movies." And he was in college, really, he was a highly educated "Negro"— and he had a fit when I told him Hannibal was black. And some of you all right now are having a fit because you didn't know it either. Hannibal was famous for crossing the Alps Mountains with elephants. Europeans couldn't go across the Alps on foot by themselves — no, they couldn't. Hannibal found a way to cross the Alps with elephants. You know what an elephant is — a great big old animal, it's hard to move him down the road. They moved him across the mountains. And he had with him 90,000 African troops, defeated Rome and occupied Italy for between 15 and 20 years.

This is why you find many Italians dark — some of that Hannibal blood. No Italian will ever jump up in my face and start putting bad mouth on me, because I know his history. I tell him when you talk about me, you're talking about your pappy, your father. He knows his history, he knows how he got that color. Don't you know that just a handful of black American troops spent a couple of years in England during World War II and left more brown babies back there — just a handful of black American soldiers in England and in Paris and in Germany messed up the whole country. Now what do you think 90,000 Africans are going to do in Italy for 20 years? It's good to know this because when you know it, you don't have to get a club to fight the man — put truth on him.

. Even the Irish got a dose of your and my blood when the Spanish Armada was defeated off the coast of Ireland, I think around about the 17th or 18th century; I forget exactly, you can check it out. The Spanish in those days were dark. They were the remnants of the Moors, and they went ashore and settled down in Ireland and right to this very day you've got what's known as the Black Irish. And it's not an accident that they call them Black Irish. If you look at them, they've got dark hair, dark features, and they've got Spanish names — like Eamon de Valera, the president, and there used to be another one called Costello. These names came from the Iberian Peninsula, which is the Spanish-Portuguese Peninsula, and they came there through these seamen, who were dark in those days. Don't let any Irishman jump up in your face and start telling you about you — why, he's got some of your blood too. You've spread your blood everywhere. If you start to talk to any one of them, I don't care where he is, if you know history, you can put him right in his place. In fact, he'll stay in his place, if he knows that you know your history.

West-African Cultures

So all of this Carthage, Sumerian, Dravidian, Egyptian, Ethiopian history took place B. C., before Christ. In this era that you and I are living in after Christ, right in West Africa, one of the most highly developed civilizations was Ghana. Ghana wasn't located where she is today geographically, she wasn't limited to that geographic location — she covered pretty much a great portion of West Africa, and dates the early history of that empire at almost up to the time of the birth of Christ. And it was a highly developed civilization, highly developed society, that prevailed right up until I think around the 11th century, or perhaps it went out of existence as an empire just before the 10th or the 11th century. But this was an empire in Africa that was the source of gold and ivory, and other art objects, what would be called today art objects or items of luxury, came from Ghana. They had one of the highest developed governmental systems, tax systems, cultures, period, at that time when people in Europe —

When President Nkrumah — he wasn't president then, I don't think — visited New York — I think it was in 1959; Harriman was Governor — they had a banquet for him downtown, which I attended. Governor Harriman, Abe Stark, Mayor Wagner, all of them were there. At one point when they were introducing Nkrumah, they were congratulating him. I remember Abe Stark said this — that Nkrumah comes from Ghana, a country which was highly civilized, wearing silks, at a time when we, he said, up in Europe, were painting ourselves blue. Pick up on that. Abe Stark at that time was right under Wagner, and he's Jewish, which means he knows a whole lot of black history, and here he was admitting that a civilization existed in Africa, where you and I came from, that was so highly developed that the people were wearing silks when his people, the Europeans, were up in the caves paint-

25

ing themselves blue. Now you would think, with him saying that, that the black newspaper reporters present would have put it in the paper and used it to wake up some of us in Harlem. They didn't say a mumbling word. And I know — I could name the ones that were there right now, some of them occupying leading positions in black newspapers in this city. They didn't say a mumbling word.

They should have put it in the headlines, so they could wake black people up, and let our people know that the white man knows that he didn't get us out of the jungle, he didn't get us out of some place that was savage — he got us out of a place that was highly civilized in culture and in art, and then brought us down to the level that you see us on today. But they are afraid to let us know what level we were on. They'll tell the Africans because they know the Africans know it, but they don't want you and me to know it. Because the first thing you and I would start asking them is, "Well, what did you do to us?" And if you find out, then you'll want to do it to him. The only way you can forgive him is to not know what you're forgiving him for. And you don't know what you've been forgiving him for. If you find out what he did to you, you won't have any forgiveness. No, you'll say let the good times roll, let the chips fall where they may.

After Ghana in West Africa, there was another civilization called Mali. Mali is one of the most famous because it was made famous by a black sultan named Mansa Musa. Mansa Musa was famed for a journey he took from Mali to Mecca.

[A few words are lost here as the tape is turned.]

In the same area — all of these three empires were in West Africa — after the Mali, I think, it was the Songhai empire. The Songhai empire covered, I think, even more territory than the Mali empire. And in those days there was the fabulous, fabled city of Timbuktu. Timbuktu was a center of learning where they had colleges and universities; and this Timbuktu existed as a hidden city, or forbidden city, to the white man for many centuries. He was not permitted to go there, none of them had been there — it was for us. They had universities there in which scholars traveled from China, Japan, the Orient, from Asia, from Africa, all the parts of Africa, to come there and learn. This was in Africa, and this existed before the discovery of America. These people who taught at this university, or these universities, had a knowledge of geography. They knew that the earth was round. It wasn't Columbus that discovered that it was round for people in Europe; they discovered it when they began to be exposed to the science and learning that existed in the universities on the African continent. But the white man is such a liar, he doesn't want it to be known that the black man was so far ahead of him in science. Now, this isn't racist talk, when I say he's a liar. I'm not talking about all of them, I'm talking about those who are responsible for this false concept of the African image, and that is most of them. If I said all of them, they'd call me a racist. I can't say all of them, but most of them, those in power, that told lies deliberately and scientifically to distort the image of Africa in order to mold a better picture and image of Europe — you can see the crime that they committed once you begin to delve into the African continent today and find its real position in science and civilization in times gone by.

Also, at that same time or a little later was a civilization called the Moors. The Moors were also a dark-skinned people on the African continent, who had a highly developed civilization. They were such magnificent warriors that they crossed the Straits of Gibraltar in, I think, the year 711, 8th century, conquered Portugal, what we today know as Portugal, Spain, and Southern France, conquered it and ruled it for seven hundred years. And they admit that during this time Europe was in "Dark Ages," meaning darkness, ignorance. And it was the only light spot; the only light, the only light of learning, that existed on the European continent at that time were the universities that the Moors had erected in what we today know as Spain and Portugal. These were African universities that they set up in that area. And they ruled throughout that area, up until a place known as Tours, where they were stopped by a Frenchman known in history as Charles Martel, or Charles the Hammer. He stopped the invasion of the Africans, and these were Africans. They try to confuse you and me by calling them Moors, so that you and I won't know what they were. But when you go home, look in the dictionary. Look up the word M-o-o-r; it will tell you that Moor means black. Well, if Negro means black and Moor means black, then they're talking about the same people all the time. But they don't want you and me to know that we were warriors, that we conquered, that we had armies; they want you and me to think that we were always non-violent, and passive, and peaceful, and forgiving. Sure, we forgave our enemies in those days — after we killed them, we forgave them.

Invention of Gunpowder

The black man in those days had never been defeated on the battlefield. He was only defeated when the Europeans invented, or got access to, gunpowder. I started to say invented gunpowder, but they didn't invent it, the Chinese invented it. The Chinese used it for peaceful purposes. Marco Polo, I think it was Marco, got ahold of it, and brought it back to Europe, and immediately they started using it to kill people with. This is the difference — that European, he's got something going for him that other people don't have going for them: He loves to kill — oh yes, he does. In Asia and in Africa, we kill for food. In Europe, they kill for sport. Have you not noticed that? Yes, they're bloodthirsty, they love blood; they love to see the flow of other people's blood, not their own. They're bloodthirsty, but in all of your ancient Asian or African societies, the killing of game was done for food, not just for sport. You don't get your kicks killing. They get their kicks killing. It gets good to them. Oh yes, you watch them sometime when they shoot a pheasant. I've watched them; when I was a little boy, I lived on a farm with white folks. When they shoot something, they just go crazy, you know, like they were really getting their kicks. And we have heard stories where they have lynched black people, and right while they were lynching that black man, you could see them getting their kicks, the thrill, while they do it. Whereas you and I, when we kill, we kill because we need to, either for food or to defend ourselves. That's something to think about.

But they never defeated the African armies until they got gunpowder. Then with their gunpowder, they came in. In those days, we had mastered the blade. Right now, you notice they have nightmares when they think a Negro's got a blade in his pocket. This is true, because they know you know how to use it, brothers. Historically, on the battlefield, no one could use a blade like you and me — yes. You see, it takes a man to use one, for one thing. It takes a man to use a sword and a spear, because you've got to have the heart to get up to someone close enough to work with him; you've got to have the heart. But anybody can take a gun and stand at a distance and shoot at something that's no danger to him anyway. You and I, we went right on into him. And once he got ahold of the gun, that suited his nature; and he used it, and took over the world, with that gunpowder and his lies — I don't know which was the most effective. He lied and killed, to take over the world.

During the Crusades, we fought him and beat him; again, he didn't have the gunpowder. During the Crusades, the Europeans fought against the Asians and the Africans — it was the war between what they called the Muslims and the Christians. In those days, you didn't have black Christians. Christians meant the European nations, France, Belgium. You go read the history of the Crusades. You'll find that their chief general was the Pope, his headquarters was in Rome, and they made war trying to redeem the city of Jerusalem, in which was the tomb of Jesus. They wanted to regain it from the Muslims, but they never could do it. The Muslims defeated the Christian armies. And the Christian armies in those days were white; the Muslim armies were black, brown, red and yellow. Some of the leading warriors in the Muslim armies were from Africa. The Africans had mastered metalwork with such skill that they had a coat that they put on, made of steel, that was just as pliable as this. Whereas, when you see the white knight, you notice he had to have some help to get on his horse? Because he looked like he was inside of a stove. They didn't know how to work metal in Europe. But that black man had mastered metalcraft, woodcraft, leathercraft — he was crafty, brothers, he mastered everything. But not a thing in Europe. And it was during the Crusades that many of the people in Europe realized what a high culture existed in Asia and in Africa. Why, these people were living in huts in Europe, and in holes in the hills, still in that day — they were savages almost, didn't know what learning was, couldn't read and write. The king couldn't even read and write, and he was over all of them. They got all their reading and writing and arithmetic from you and me. And you see what they did with it? They turned around and used it on us.

So the question is, if we were at such a level then, what happened to us to get us where we are now? If we had such a high culture, such a high civilization, what happened to get us where we are now?

When America was discovered and colonized by England, England populated her American colonies not with people who were refined and cultured, but, if you read the history, she did the same thing here that she did in Australia. All the convicts were sent here to found this country. The prisons were emptied of prostitutes and thieves and murderers. They were sent over here to populate this country. When these people jump up in your and my face today, talking about [how] the founding fathers were puritan pure, that's some talk for somebody else. No, the founding fathers from England came from the dungeons of England, came from the prisons of England; they were prostitutes, they were murderers and thieves and liars. And as soon as they got over here, they proved it. They created one of the most criminal societies that has ever existed on the earth since time began. And, if you doubt it, when you go home at night, look in the mirror at yourself, and you'll see the victim of that criminal system that was created by them.

They were such artful liars, they were such artful, skillful liars, that they were able to take a criminal system and, with lies, project it to the world as a humanitarian system. They were the worst form of criminals themselves, but with their lies they were able to project themselves as pilgrims who were so religious they were coming to this country so they could practice their religion. And you ate that thing up 100 per cent. No, they were crooks that came here — Washington, Jefferson, Adams, Quincy and the others, all of them were criminals. And if you doubt that they were, when they wrote this document talking about freedom, they still owned you. Yes, when they wrote, how does that thing go — about "all men created equal"? — that was later on. Who was it wrote that — "all men created equal"? It was Jefferson. Jefferson had more slaves than anybody else. So they weren't talking about us. When I see some poor old brainwashed Negroes — [if] you mention Thomas Jefferson and George Washington and Patrick Henry, they just swoon, you know, with patriotism. But they don't realize that in the sight of George Washington, you were a sack of molasses, a sack of potatoes. You, yes, were a sack of potatoes, a barrel of molasses, you amounted to nothing, in the sight of Washington, or in the sight of Jefferson, or Hamilton, and some of those other so-called founding fathers. You were their property. And if it was left up to them, you'd still be their property today.

American Slavery

So it was in that atmosphere that you and I arrived here. It was in the hands of that kind of people that you and I fell, in around the 16th century. When we came here as slaves, we were civilized, we had culture, we had a knowledge of science. They don't take a slave who's dumb — a dumb slave is not good, you have to know how to do something to be a profitable slave. This was a country that needed an agricultural system. They had no agriculture in Europe in the 15th and 16th centuries. What was the agricultural product, what farm product was Europe famous for? Tell me — you can't, they had none, they were growing weeds up there in Europe. The farm products, the agricultural system, existed in Africa and Asia. You had mastered the growing of cotton, you had mastered the growing of all of the farm products that are necessary to give a person a balanced diet, on the African continent. You were a master of woodcraft, metalwork and all of these other skills; and it was this that they needed. They didn't need just someone with muscle to do work — they needed someone with skill. So they brought our people here, who were the fathers of skill, who had all of these skills. And they brought us here to set up an agricultural system for them, to weave their clothes, and show them how to weave, and do the other things that make a civilization and society a balanced civilization and society.

So when our people got here — and they came here from a civilization where they had high morals; there was no stealing, no drunkenness, no adultery, fornication; there was nothing but high morals — when they got here, they found a country that had the lowest morals that existed on earth at that time, because it was peopled and run by prostitutes, by cutthroats, by criminals; and they created a society to fit their

31

nature. And when our people came into that, they were shocked — they rebelled against it, they didn't want to stay here. In the first place, they had been tricked over here, put in chains and brought here, as history points out. Initially -there's a book called *The Slave Trade* by Spears* in which it points out that one of the first slave ships to come here was piloted by an Englishman named John Hawkins, and John Hawkins' ship was called Jesus, the good ship Jesus. This was the boat that was used — it's in history — they used Jesus to bring them here. And then used him to keep you here, too.

When our people got here and found out what they had gotten into, they didn't want to stay. Many of them started looking for that ship that brought them here. The slaves had an old spiritual which they sang: "Steal away to Jesus, steal away home." You think that they were talking about some man that got hung on the cross two thousand years ago, whereas they were talking about a ship. They wanted to steal away and get on board that ship that was named Jesus, so that they could go back home on the mother continent, the African continent, where they had been tricked and brought from. But you've got poor Negroes today, who have been brainwashed, still sitting in church talking about stealing away to Jesus; they talk about going up yonder, dying, if they're going somewhere. Showing you how your mind is all messed up. They were talking about a boat.

Or, they used to sing a song, "You can have all this world, but give me Jesus." They weren't talking about that man that died supposedly on the cross, they were talking about a boat. "You can have this world" — this Western world, this evil, corrupt, run-down, low-down Western world — but give me Jesus the boat, but give me the ship Jesus, so I can go back home where I'll be among my own kind. This is what the spiritual came from. But they've got it in the church today, and that old dumb preacher has your and my — yes, dumb preacher — has your and my mind so messed up we think that Jesus is somebody that died on a cross, and we sit there foaming at the mouth talking about you can have all this world, but give me Jesus. And the man took all this world, and gave you Jesus, and that's all you've got is Jesus.

* *The American Slave Trade, An Account of its Origin, Growth and Suppression,* John Randolph Spears. Scribners, 1900.

There were three people involved in the crime that was committed against us — the slave trader, the slave master, and a third one that they don't tell you and me about, the slave maker. You've read about the slave trader and you've read about the slave master; in fact, you know the slave master — you're still in his hands. But you never read in history the part played by the slave maker. You can't make a wise man a slave, you can't make a warrior a slave. When you and I came here, or rather when we were brought here, we were brought here from a society that was highly civilized, our culture was at the highest level, and we were warriors — we knew no fear. How could they make us slaves? They had to do the same thing to us that we do to a horse. When you take a horse out of the wilds, you don't just jump on him and ride him, or put a bit in his mouth and use him to plow with. No, you've got to break him in first. Once you break him in, then you can ride him. Now the man who rides him is not the man who breaks him in. It takes a different type of man to break him in than it takes to ride him. The average man that's been riding him can't break him in. It takes a cruel man to break him in, a mean man, a heartless man, a man with no feelings. And this is why they took the role of the slave maker out of history. It was so criminal that they don't even dare to write about it, to tell what was done to you and me to break us in and break us down to the level that we're on today. Because if you find the role that that slave maker played, I'm telling you, you'll find it hard to forget and forgive, you'll find it hard. I can't forgive the slave trader or the slave master; you know I can't forgive the slave maker.

Slave Making

Our people weren't brought right here to this country. They were first dropped off in the West Indian islands, in the Caribbean. Most of the slaves that were brought from Africa were dropped off first in the Caribbean, West Indian islands. Why? This was the breaking-in grounds. They would break them in down there. When they broke them in, then they would bring the ones whose spirit had been broken on to America. They had all kinds of tactics for breaking them in. They

33

bred fear into them, for one thing. I read in one book how the slave maker used to take a pregnant woman, a black woman, and make her watch as her man would be tortured and put to death. One of those slave makers had trees that he planted in positions where he would bend them and tie them, and then tie the hand of a black man to one, a hand to the other, and his legs to two more, and he'd cut the rope. And when he'd cut the rope, that tree would snap up and pull the arm of the black man right out of his socket, pull him up into four different parts. I'll show you books where you can read it, they write about it. And they made the pregnant black women stand there and watch as they did it, so that all this grief and fear that they felt would go right into that baby, that black baby that was yet to be born. It would be born afraid, born with fear in it. And you've got it in you right now — right now, you've still got it. When you get in front of that blue-eyed thing, you start to itching, don't you? And you don't know why. It was bred into you. But when you find out how they did it, you can get it out of you and put it right back in them.

Now, I'm not talking racism. This isn't racism — this is history, we're dealing with just a little bit of history tonight. We've only got a few minutes left, so I'm trying to go fast. I'm kind of tired, so I can't go too fast — you'll have to excuse me — but I just want to get the rest of this out.

They used to take a black woman who would be pregnant and tie her up by her toes, let her be hanging head down, and they would take a knife and cut her stomach open, let that black unborn child fall out, and then stomp its head in the ground. I'll show you books where they write about this, I'll name them to you: *Slave Trade* by Spears; *From Slavery to Freedom* by John Hope Franklin; *Negro Family in the U. S.* by Frazier touches on some of it. All night long — *Anti-Slavery* by Dwight Lowell Dumond — I'll cite you books all night long, where they write themselves on what they did to you and me. And have got the nerve to say we teach hate because we're talking about what they did. Why, they're lucky, really, they're lucky, they're fortunate.

Slaves used to sing that song about "My Lord's going to move this wicked race and raise up a righteous nation that will obey." They knew what they were talking about — they were talking about the man. They used to sing a song, "Good news, a chariot is coming." If you notice, everything they sang in those spirituals was talking about going to get away from here. None of them wanted to stay here. You're the only ones, sitting around here now like a knot on a log, wanting to stay here. You're supposed to be educated and hip, you're supposed to know what's happening, you know— they're not supposed to know what's happening. But everything they sang, every song, had a hint in it that they weren't satisfied here, that they weren't being treated right, that somebody had to go.

The slave maker knew that he couldn't make these people slaves until he first made them dumb. And one of the best ways to make a man dumb is to take his tongue, take his language. A man who can't talk, what do they call him?— a dummy. Once your language is gone, you are a dummy. You can't communicate with people who are your relatives, you can never have access to information from your family— you just can't communicate. Also, if you'll notice, the natural tongue that one speaks is referred to as one's mother tongue— mother tongue. And the natural intelligence that a person has before he goes to school is called mother wit. Not father wit—it's called mother wit because everything a child knows before it gets to school, it learns from its mother, not its father. And if it never goes to school, whatever native intelligence it has, it got it primarily from its mother, not its father; so it's called mother wit. And the mother is also the one who teaches the child how to speak its language, so that the natural tongue is called the mother tongue. Whenever you find as many people as we who aren't able to speak any mother tongue, why, that's evidence right there something was done to our mother. Something had to have happened to her.

They had laws in those days that made it mandatory for a black child to be taken from its mother as fast as that child was born. The mother never had a chance to rear it. The child would be brought up somewhere else away from the mother, so that the mother couldn't teach the child what she knew—about itself, about her past, about its heritage. It would have to grow up in complete darkness, knowing nothing about the land where it came from or the people that it came from. Not even about its own mother. There was no relationship between the black child and its mother; it was against the law. And if the master would ever find any of those children who had any knowledge of its mother tongue, that child was put to death. They had to stamp out the language; they did it scientifically. If they found any one of them that could speak it, off went its head, or they would ˹ut it to death, they would kill it, in front of the mother, if ˸essary. This is history; this is how they took your lan- ˴age. You didn't lose it, it didn't evaporate — they took it with a scientific process, because they knew they had to take it to make you dumb, or into the dummy that you and I now are.

I read in some books where it said that some of the slave mothers would try and get tricky. In order to teach their child, who'd be off in another field somewhere, they themselves would be praying and they'd pray in a loud voice, and in their own language. The child in the distant field would hear his mother's voice, and he'd learn how to pray in the same way; and in learning how to pray, he'd pick up on some of the language. And the master found that this was being done, and immediately he stepped up his efforts to kill all the little children that were benefitting from this. And so it became against the law even for the slave to be caught praying in his tongue, if he knew it. It was against the law. You've heard some of the people say they had to pray with their heads in a bucket. Well, they weren't praying to the Jesus that they're praying to now. The white man will let you call on that Jesus all day long; in fact he'll make it possible for you to call on him. If you were calling on somebody else, then he'd have more fear of it. You're calling on that somebody else in that other language — that causes him a bit of fear, a bit of fright.

They used to have to steal away and pray. All those songs that the slaves talked, or sang, and called spirituals, had wrapped up in them some of what was happening to them. And when the child realized that it couldn't hear its mother pray any more, the slaves would come up with a song, "I couldn't hear nobody pray," or the song, "Motherless Child"— "Sometimes, I feel like a motherless child. Father gone, mother gone, motherless child sees a hard time." All of these songs were describing what was happening to us then, in the only way the slaves knew how to communicate—in song. They didn't dare say it outright, so they put it in song. They pretended that they were singing about Moses in "Go down, Moses"—they weren't talking about Moses and telling "old Pharaoh to let my people go." They were trying to talk some kind of talk to each other, over the slave master's head. Now you've got ahold of the thing and you're believing in it for real. Yes, I hear you singing "Go down, Moses" and you're still talking about Moses four thousand years ago—you're out of your mind. But those slaves had a whole lot of sense. Everything they sang was designed toward freedom, designed toward going back home, or designed toward getting this big white ape off their backs.

The Main Lesson

For three hundred years, we stayed at that level. Finally, we got to where we had no language, no history, no name. The white man named us after himself—Jones, Smith, Johnson, Bunche, and names like those. We couldn't speak our own language; we had none. And he then began to teach us that we came from a jungle, where the people had no language. This was the crime that was committed—he convinced us that our people back home were savages and animals in the jungle, and the reason we couldn't talk was because we never had a language. And we grew up thinking that we never had one.

In the meantime, while he was working on us, his brothers, in England and in France and in Belgium and in Spain and in Italy and in Germany, were working on the African continent. While he was working on us over here, they were running wild on the African continent, stomping out all signs that ever there was a civilization over there, making slaves out of them over there too. And by working together as partners, the man on the European continent, in cahoots with this white man on the American continent, succeeded in taking over Africa and Asia and the entire world, while we went to sleep.

Then in 1865 he came up with a trick, pretending that he was fighting a civil war to set us free—which wasn't to set us free. He came up with another trick, that he was issuing an emancipation proclamation to set us free — which wasn't to set us free. And then he also pretended that he was putting some amendments to the Constitution to set us free — which wasn't to set us free. Later on, he came up with a Supreme Court decision which he said was to give us free access to better education — which wasn't to do that. And then last year he came up with a bill that he called also to give us more freedom — which also wasn't to do that.

Any man who will know the level of civilization that we started out on, and came from, any man who knows the criminal deeds that were done to us by his people to bring us to the level that we've been on for the past three hundred years, knows he is so deceptive, so deceitful, so criminally deceitful, that it is almost beyond his nature or desire to come up with anything meaningful that will undo what has been done to us over the past three hundred years. It is absolutely necessary — anything that is done for us, has to be done by us.

Now, brothers and sisters, it's after ten o'clock, and I definitely didn't intend to go beyond ten, but I do want you to have at least a ten-minute question period before we dismiss and prepare for our meeting next week. I felt that it was necessary tonight to go back somewhat and remind ourselves — because many of you know everything that I have said tonight, you know it already; then there are many others who don't — but I felt it absolutely necessary to use tonight, since we're getting ready to go into February and Negro History Week, to use tonight to kind of brush up on some of the history of our people that existed prior to the time we were brought to America; then next week, next Sunday night, deal with current conditions and the tricky schemes that are used by the government as well as other forces to perpetuate our condition, rather than alleviate it. And then on the third Sunday, the 31st of January, it is our intention to present to you the program and the solution of the Organization of Afro-American Unity, which we feel will bring about some meaningful results immediately, and which we will ask your 100 per cent cooperation in, in order to make it materialize.

Before we have our question period, we're going to take up a collection. And I want to ask you, especially tonight, please be more generous than you have been. Because if there's anything we need, it's finances. We don't get any help from any outside source. Anybody else would get it. We don't get any help whatsoever other than what we get right here at these meetings from you. Also, this week we want to take out an ad in one of the local newspapers, so that it will be known that we're out here next week. None of the newspapers ever talk about our meetings; they don't help us publicize it in any way, shape, or form, other than *The Militant*— *The Militant* does. But some of the Negro newspapers don't; I don't know whether they won't, but I do know that they don't. And I would like for you to try and dig down as deeply as you can and help us. Because we need it. In fact, if we could get stronger financial support, we'd be in a position to make our program materialize much faster than we have.

[Collection is taken.]

(A question is asked by a woman about the selling of slaves by Africans to the Europeans.)

Malcolm: All of those things happened. Africans sold slaves; we sold each other. Arabs sold slaves. The white man bought the slaves. You may wonder what happened to make us sell each other. The white man had a trick going— what he called the three something-or-other. It dealt with rum, sugar cane— how does that go? They would grow sugar cane in the Caribbean and take it to New England and turn it into rum, and then take that rum to Africa and turn it into slaves. It was something like that. [*Voices from audience: "Triangular."*] How was that? Yeah, triangle, some kind of triangle. Imagine that, they used our slave labor to grow the sugar cane; they took that cane to England and turned it into rum and whiskey and other things, and then took that to Africa and turned it into slaves. And then they had cotton that they took to Europe in exchange for manufactured goods that were being turned out there. But you and I, our sale, is what made them rich.

Now, who did it? The Africans took captives in warfare, and the Europeans did that old divide-and-conquer act, and would sell guns to one side; and the guns that the one side had, enabled them to easily defeat the other side. And in that particular cultural thought-pattern, the captive was a slave, he was a prize of war, and he was turned over to the Europeans. I doubt that any of them over there really knew what they were sending us into, or that we knew what we were coming into. But it was a very vicious thing; you and I are the victims of it. Everybody feels guilty about it, you can believe it. The Arabs are guilty; Europeans are guilty; the Africans feel guilty; everybody feels guilty. Yes, sir.

(A question is asked by a man about the different kinds of slavery that existed at different times in different countries.)
Malcolm: Yes, and I'm glad you brought that out. It is true that the type of slavery that was practiced in America was never practiced in history by any other country. A lot of times, what you read about in history as a slave was nothing but a servant, because he could get out of it. But the thing that you and I were sold into — we were sold like we were an animal. Our human characteristics were not recognized at all. We became a commodity, nameless, languageless, godless commodity, subhuman. And they had no feelings for us whatsoever. In church, they did it in the name of the Lord. Oh yes, they even put that into it. And don't say anything about that church in Rome — they played one of the leading roles. Now, they try to act all sanctimonious, you know, like everything is all right. They made a few black cardinals, a couple other bishops, and then you run and get the Catholic Holy Ghost. Any more questions? Yes, sir.

(A question is asked by a man about the relationship between the people that brought the slaves to America and "the people that rule us today.")
Malcolm: Oh yes, their descendants. That's all they are, brother, believe me. This is what makes them so deceitful, and tricky. Like father, like son. You and I were produced by kings and queens from the African continent, scientists, the best. They took the best of the African society, and sold them as slaves. We brought the highest price. We didn't come here as chumps; we were the cream of the crop on the African continent. But not those men. Those that were sent here from Europe were the dregs of society. Old, run-down, ex-, worn-out — thieves; you thought I was going to say something else, didn't you? No, they were the worst part of that

European society, brother, and they still reflect it right today.

Everything you see them doing here—no feelings; they'll sell you right down the river right now. They have no morals at all; no sense of moral consciousness exists in them. They will lie, talk about the Great Society, and all that other stuff. No, nothing but lies. How is somebody from Texas going to start a great society? They don't have it down there. You know back, when I was out there in the world, I used to see Willie Bryant at the Apollo. You remember Willie Bryant? They had a song in those days about "Deep in the Heart of Texas," and I used to hear Willie Bryant singing, "The stars are bright, they'll hang you any night, deep in the heart of Texas." This is just twenty years ago, and they still do the same thing today. And Johnson was congressman then. You know Johnson—he's got a cold. Are there any other questions? Yes, sir.

(A question is asked by a man about the number of Indians left in the United States.)

Malcolm: Indians? He's on the reservation. They put me and you on the plantation, and put the Indians on the reservation—that's how they built this nation. The Indian is in worse shape than we are. I was out in the desert at an Arizona reservation a couple of years ago. They're in bad shape. But they have more respect for the Indians than they do for you and me. You know why? Because they fought them. You don't hear any white man talking about he's got black trouble, but in a minute you'll hear him say he's got some Indian trouble. A white man will say that. Haven't you heard it? Sure, they'll claim the Indians, but nobody is going to claim you and me—because we're non-violent. Nobody wants to be related to anything non-violent, nobody. You're going to be a peaceful slave, a non-violent slave. No, that Indian, brother, he drank blood; he tomahawked. Imagine taking a man's scalp, and then he's going to say he's got your blood? He'll respect you. No, that's what you need to learn how to do. The Indians said they had forked tongues, which means they're liars, you know. The Indians knew them. And they show you every time you turn on the television—any old cowboy picture shows you a white man lying to the Indian. He doesn't hide it. Time for a couple more questions, a couple more questions. Any more? Yes, ma'am.

(A question is asked by a woman about "the slave breeder.")

Malcolm: No, the slave breeder was that slave maker. The slave maker was the one responsible for breeding slaves, and he bred them. They bred any kind of looking slave you wanted.

(Same woman speaks further, referring to the novel, Mandingo.)

Malcolm: Yes. I know some of you all never read *Mandingo,* did you? It is true that they used to have special black slaves that they called bucks, I think, whose job was to do nothing but breed. I see a lot of them, I think, around Harlem now. In those days a child born of a slave woman never knew its father, didn't know who the father was; didn't make any difference. And, you know, this has affected our society.

Even right now you read some of the conclusions reached by some of these so-called sociologists. They admit that the tendency of our women to have babies, born out of wedlock, is a throwback right to a habit that was born during slavery. In slavery, it was nothing for a black woman to have a baby—she was supposed to have a baby. And the father, the black man who fathered the baby, was never permitted to have the responsibility of a father. All he did was make the baby. He couldn't recognize it as his; it was going to be sold as soon as the master wanted to sell it. He was never permitted to develop a sense of responsibility for taking care of his own offspring. And that came right down through slavery to the black community today. You'll find many men who are married and have two or three children, walk away from that woman like she didn't even exist, and leave those children in the house without a second thought, without a second thought. Well, you wouldn't find an African doing this. We weren't like this in Africa. This is a throwback, this is a holdover, from slavery. We've got to get rid of it. But you're never going to get rid of it until you get rid of the cause, and, man, you know who the cause is. Are there any other questions?

Then I have some announcements that I would like to read quickly. Our newsletter, *The Blacklash,* is going to be revised and turned into a newspaper, a more informative and attractive newspaper. We're working on that right now. And the brother who has been doing such a wonderful job on the newsletter is Brother Peter. I don't see him — where is Brother Peter? Way back there, the handsome brother. Give him a big hand. He's been doing a wonderful job on the newsletter, and he's now working toward turning it into a newspaper.

Also, there'll be a membership meeting of the Organization of Afro-American Unity, Tuesday, January 26, at 8:00 p.m., at 2395 8th Avenue. We would like all of the members to attend, because we're trying to get ourselves organized in such a way that we can become inseparably involved in an action program that will meet the needs, desires, likes, or dislikes of everyone that's involved. And we want you involved in it. Also, the aims and the objectives of the Organization of Afro-American Unity are being prepared right now. They will be made available soon. We are attempting to make this organization one in which any serious-minded Afro-American can actively participate, and we welcome your suggestions at all of these membership meetings. One of these will be on Tuesday night. We want your suggestions; we don't in any way claim to have the answers to everything, but we do feel that all of us combined can come up with an answer. We believe that the brain that you have, the ability to think, your experience in this hell that we've all been through, is all the credentials you need when you come to a membership meeting with your suggestions. With all of the combined suggestions and the combined talent and know-how, we do believe that we can devise a program that will shake the world. Frankly, that's what we need to do — shake the world. We don't need to duplicate anything that has been done with all this politeness and compromise and so forth; we need to find out what is necessary to be done, and do it, no matter whether they like it or not. First, analyze it, find out what is necessary to be done, and then let's do it. Yes, sir.

(A man asks about a telegram that was to be sent to the leader of the American Nazi Party.)

Malcolm: Let me see if I have it here. I sent this telegram to Rockwell the other day. It states: to George Lincoln Rockwell, "This is to warn you that I am no longer held in check from fighting white supremacists by Elijah Muhammad's separationist Black Muslim movement, and that if your present racist agitation against our people there in Alabama causes physical harm to Reverend King or any other black Americans who are only attempting to enjoy their rights as free human beings, that you and your Ku Klux Klan friends will be met with maximum physical retaliation from those of us who are not handcuffed by the disarming philosophy of non-violence, and who believe in asserting our right of self-defense by any means necessary."

That was sent. And it was sent at a time when he was acting bad and bogish there in Selma. And you haven't heard anything about it since. No. The entire press was aware that it was sent. Nothing about it; they wouldn't print it. I'm going to tell you why they wouldn't print it, and I must tell you. The so-called liberal element of the white power structure never wants to see nationalists involved in anything that has to do with civil rights. And I'll tell you why. Any other black people who get involved are involved within the rules that are laid down by the white liberals. And as long as they are involved within those rules, then that means they're only going to go as far as the liberal element of the power structure will endorse their activity. But when the nationalistic-minded blacks get involved, then we do what our analysis tells us is necessary to be done, whether the white liberal or anybody else likes it or not. So, they don't want us involved.

Plus, I was curious to find out how Dr. King would react, if he were told. See, I saw him getting knocked down on television, I saw the man knock him in his mouth. Well, that hurt me, I'll tell you. Because I'm black and he's black — I don't care how dumb he is. Still, when I see a black man knocked in the mouth, I feel it, because it could happen to you or me. And if I was there with King and I saw someone knocking on him, I'd come to his rescue. I would be misrepresenting myself if I made you think I wouldn't. Yes, and then I'd show him, see, he's doing it the wrong way—this is the way you do it. Did you have more to that, sir?

(A man relates an incident, following the attempted World's Fair stall-in during April, 1964, when Roy Wilkins and the NAACP national office cracked down on an NAACP youth council that had wanted to invite a black nationalist speaker.)

Malcolm: Yes. You know why, brother? Because they are afraid, as I say for any nationalist-minded person to get involved with any civil rights Negro. See, the civil-rights Negro—let me use the word Negro for a minute—the civil-rights Negro is in a straitjacket. Really, he is. Read this book, *The Negro Mood*—the chapter, "The Black Establishment"—and you'll see they're in a straitjacket. I'll tell you frankly what I intend to do. Since they used to condemn me all the time, when I was in the Black Muslim movement, for talking but not getting involved, "Okay," I'll say, "you've got some action going? I'll get involved, I'll get involved." But I know they don't want me involved. Because if I get involved, I'm for involvement all the way.

I say this, that if the law of the land states that you and I have the right to do thus and so, it doesn't take a picket to establish that right. All we've got to do is go and do it. Now, anyone who gets in our way to deprive us of that right which is constitutional—Supreme Court and all that kind of stuff—anyone who gets in our way is a law-breaker. We're not the law-breakers; we're enforcing the law. Anyone who stops you from trying to register and vote is breaking the law. You can waste him, yes, you can waste him, and there's nothing he can do about it. Now they know this. This is why they want to keep you out of the civil rights struggle. They don't want any nationalists involved.

And you actually do the whole thing a disservice by not getting involved, because what you do is create a vacuum, into which steps Uncle Tom. And Uncle Tom takes all the black belts and leads them the non-violent way. No, I say let's all get in it, and get in it without compromise, and anybody that gets in the way—don't compromise. That's all. If black people in Alabama are trying to register and vote, if they're trying to register, then those black people in Alabama are within their rights. Anyone who in any way interferes with them is breaking the law. Well, our people in Alabama, our people in Harlem, our people in California are the same people. You and I will not get anywhere by standing on the sidelines, saying they're doing it wrong. I spent twelve years doing this in the Black Muslim movement, condemning everybody walking, and at no time were we permitted to get involved to show a better way. Okay, I say let's get involved. But let's get involved all the way. Let's don't get involved in a compromise way. That doesn't mean we're going to get involved in just anything. But a man has a right to vote, a man has a right to be registered. In areas especially in the South where our people outnumber whites, if they were registered they could put all the whites out of office.

But you know, this is between you and me, I just want to say — between you and me, and the stoolpigeons present — even here in Harlem, where we have the right to register and vote, we don't register and vote. If all the people in Alabama could register and vote, they probably wouldn't register and vote. So, you see, you have to have a multiple program, a many-pronged program. And so when I say that we're for that, that doesn't mean that we're not for some other things, too. It takes a many-pronged program to get this problem solved.

But, brothers, the man can't give you the solution. You never will get the solution from any white liberal. Let you and I sit down and discuss the problem, come up with what we feel the solution will be; and then if they want to help it, then let them help in their way, in a way that they can help. But don't let them come and tell us how we should do to solve our problem. Those days are over, I can't see that at all. If they want to help in their way, a way that they can help, good; but don't come and join us and try and sit down and tell us how to solve our problem. They can't do it, and they won't. That's like asking the fox to help you solve the problem confronting you and the wolf. He'll tell you how to solve it all right, but I'll guarantee you, you'll have a worse problem afterwards — a foxy problem. He'll give you a solution that will put you right in his clutches; and this is what the white liberal does.

Very seldom, if you notice, will you find whites who can in any way put up with black nationalists. Haven't you ever wondered why? I mean even the most liberal white can't go along with this black nationalism. He can't, he just can't stomach it. But he can go along with anything that's integrated, because he knows he can get in there and finagle it, and have you walking backwards, thinking you're walking forwards. No, we don't want that. There's a place for them, there's some work that they can do. I'm not saying cut them out — there's something that they can do. But I say, find out what the whites can do, and let them do that; and find out what we can do, and we'll do that. Let them go their way; you take the low road and we'll take the high road, and so on and so forth.

Also, a couple more announcements, please. We're having an Arabic class beginning tomorrow, Monday, January 25, at 7 p.m.—tomorrow evening—in Room 128 at the Hotel Theresa. We're having classes set up in Swahili—we have one set up already in Arabic—we're having one set up in Swahili, and another one in Hausa, so that you can be, what they call it, multi-lingual. You know, one of the things I found out when I was in Africa, I felt very much at a loss, many times, by not being able to speak the language. Sir? Oh, that's coming. The brother wanted to know what about a karate class. This is one of the first classes you should have—karate.

You know, I had some people try to jump on me night before last—some of those, I call them, I've got another name for them. They were waiting for me out near my house. So when I came out—thanks to Allah for good intuition—and I did some things, and they jumped me. That's right, when you read in the paper about these old crazy people going crazy, that's not any exaggeration. They even shot a brother up here in the Bronx, I think in broad daylight; and whipped another one almost dead in Boston—you probably heard him on the Barry Gray show telling about it. Well, they've gone out of their minds, absolutely. Whenever you find an organization that's equipped like that, and you never see it take part in any kind of action that's for the good of black people against the real enemy, but they will turn all of their anger against each other, to destroy each other, why, you've got to start really analyzing the situation.

I hate to bring that up, but it's true. A very bad situation has set in and deteriorated to the point where you have black people trying to kill black people; and they should be using that talent, really, to go after the Rockwells and the Klan. And you know, frankly, the more I talk about Rockwell and the Klan, the more it infuriates them—not Rockwell and the Klan, but *them*. One of these days, I'll tell you why. You'll never read anything in the Black Muslim newspaper against the Ku Klux Klan or Rockwell. You never will, not even accidentally. But if you'll go back into some of the back issues, you'll find J. P. Stoner interviewed in the Black Muslim newspaper, and he was interviewed objectively, favorably. That's not an accident, and like I say, if you keep pressing me, I'll tell you why. [*Voices from the audience: "Why?" "All right!"*]

Also, since you know that it's almost impossible for us to get the cooperation of the press in getting our meetings publicized, the only way that people in Harlem will know that we're having meetings is if you inform them. So, if each of you here right now will take it upon yourself to inform just ten people between now and Sunday, that means by next Sunday, we'll have — look at the crowd we have out here, and it's the worst kind of weather outside; it's a miracle really. You don't know, you're great. Do you know that this audience right here can whip any audience in New York City? You know why? You're game to come out there in all that mean weather. You've got all the excuse in the world to stay home tonight. But the fact that you've come out shows you're doing a whole lot of thinking about something. And I tell you, I love you for it. And I hope and pray to Allah — and whoever you believe in, whatever you believe in — I hope and pray that we'll be able to organize ourselves together, wherein we'll do anything we want, anything *we* want, to undertake in this organization. And we're working toward that end right now.

I think I've read all these announcements. James, if I — oh, yes, the last one they handed me is this: As you know, it costs us $150 to rent this hall each Sunday night, and we just collected $135. Plus, this week we had the cost of handbills and other things that we had to undertake to try and let you know where we are. So, should I turn you loose right now or pick up another collection? [*Voices from audience: "Take it, take a collection."*] I think I'd better. I hate to be like an old preacher, but brothers, I know what we're up against. We're trying to have two more meetings — don't run yet, just stay time enough — we're trying to have two more meetings, we're going to try to have a meeting next Sunday and the following Sunday. Now, within the next two weeks we are going to try and put together an organization and a program that everybody in here can participate in. But honestly — you know I wouldn't tell you this if it wasn't true — we need your help. And the only way the organization . . .

[*Tape ends here.*]

(Top) Part of an Egyptian tomb painting: whites are thought to be slaves being given to the Pharaoh by emissaries of Ethiopian king.
(Left) Black Egyptian queen, Nefertari, with her husband Aahmes I.
(Right) Painting of importantly clothed man in tomb of Rameses IV.

(Top) Royal pyramids at Meroe, ancient capital of southern Ethiopia.
(Bottom) Ruins of Temple of Naga, Kush, Ethiopia.

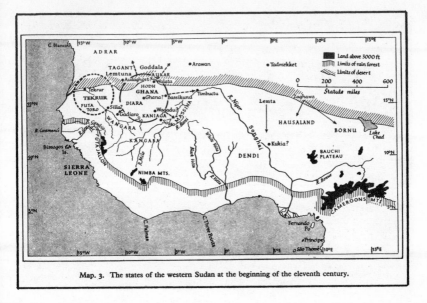

Map. 3. The states of the western Sudan at the beginning of the eleventh century.

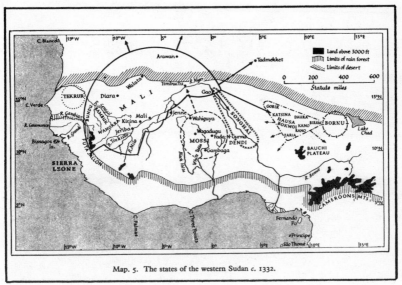

Map. 5. The states of the western Sudan c. 1332.

(Top) The states of West Africa at the start of the eleventh century.

(Bottom) The states of West Africa around 1332, the year of Mansa Musa's death.

51

(Top) Ancient palace wall at Zimbabwe, Southern Rhodesia. This wall contained 15,000 tons of stone.
(Bottom) Ancient ruins at Naletale, Southern Rhodesia.

HOW MALCOLM X STUDIED AFRO-AMERICAN HISTORY

Norfolk Prison Colony's library was one of its outstanding features. A millionaire named Parkhurst had willed his library there; he had probably been interested in the rehabilitation program. History and religions were his special interests. Thousands of his books were on the shelves, and in the back were boxes and crates full, for which there wasn't space on the shelves. At Norfolk, we could actually go into the library, with permission — walk up and down the shelves, pick books. There were hundreds of old volumes, some of them probably quite rare. I read aimlessly, until I learned to read selectively, with a purpose. . . .*

I can remember accurately the very first set of books that really impressed me. I have since bought that set of books and I have it at home for my children to read as they grow up. It's called *Wonders of the World*. It's full of pictures of archeological finds, statues that depict, usually, non-European people.

I found books like Will Durant's *Story of Civilization*. I read H. G. Wells' *Outline of History*. *Souls of Black Folk* by W. E. B. Du Bois gave me a glimpse into the black people's history before they came to this country. Carter G. Woodson's *Negro History* opened my eyes about black empires before the black slave was brought to the United States, and the early Negro struggles for freedom.

J. A. Rogers' three volumes of *Sex and Race* told about race-mixing before Christ's time; about Aesop being a black man who told fables; about Egypt's Pharaohs; about the great Coptic Christian Empires; about Ethiopia, the earth's oldest continuous black civilization, as China is the oldest continuous civilization. . . .

I never will forget how shocked I was when I began read-

---

* *The Autobiography of Malcolm X*. With the assistance of Alex Haley. Grove Press, New York, 1965, pp. 158-159.

ing about slavery's total horror. It made such an impact upon me that it later became one of my favorite subjects when I became a minister of Mr. Muhammad's. The world's most monstrous crime, the sin and the blood on the white man's hands, are almost impossible to believe. Books like the one by Frederick Olmstead opened my eyes to the horrors suffered when the slave was landed in the United States. The European woman, Fannie Kimball [Kemble], who had married a Southern white slaveowner, described how human beings were degraded. Of course I read *Uncle Tom's Cabin.* In fact, I believe that's the only novel I have ever read since I started serious reading.

Parkhurst's collection also contained some bound pamphlets of the Abolitionist Anti-Slavery Society of New England. I read descriptions of atrocities, saw those illustrations of black slave women tied up and flogged with whips; of black mothers watching their babies being dragged off, never to be seen by their mothers again; of dogs after slaves, and of the fugitive slave catchers, evil white men with whips and clubs and chains and guns. I read about the slave preacher Nat Turner, who put the fear of God into the white slave-master. Nat Turner wasn't going around preaching pie-in-the-sky and "non-violent" freedom for the black man. There in Virginia one night in 1831, Nat and seven other slaves started out at his master's home and through the night they went from one plantation "big house" to the next, killing, until by the next morning 57 white people were dead and Nat had about 70 slaves following him. White people, terrified for their lives, fled from their homes, locked themselves up in public buildings, hid in the woods, and some even left the state. A small army of soldiers took two months to catch and hang Nat Turner. Somewhere I have read where Nat Turner's example is said to have inspired John Brown to invade Virginia and attack Harper's Ferry nearly thirty years later, with thirteen white men and five Negroes....

Book after book showed me how the white man had brought upon the world's black, brown, red, and yellow peoples every variety of the sufferings of exploitation. I saw how since the sixteenth century, the so-called "Christian trader" white man began to ply the seas in his lust for Asian and African empires, and plunder, and power. I read, I saw, how the white man never has gone among the non-white peoples bearing the Cross in the true manner and spirit of Christ's teachings — meek, humble, and Christlike.

I perceived, as I read, how the collective white man had been actually nothing but a piratical opportunist who used Faustian machinations to make his own Christianity his initial wedge in criminal conquests. First, always "religiously," he branded "heathen" and "pagan" labels upon ancient non-white cultures and civilizations. The stage thus set, he then turned upon his non-white victims his weapons of war. . . .

Over 115 million African blacks — close to the 1930's population of the United States — were murdered or enslaved during the slave trade. And I read how when the slave market was glutted, the cannibalistic white powers of Europe next carved up, as their colonies, the richest areas of the black continent. And Europe's chancelleries for the next century played a chess game of naked exploitation and power from Cape Horn to Cairo. . . .*

I'll tell you something. The whole stream of Western philosophy has now wound up in a cul-de-sac. The white man has perpetrated upon himself, as well as upon the black man, so gigantic a fraud that he has put himself into a crack. He did it through his elaborate, neurotic necessity to hide the black man's true role in history.

And today the white man is faced head on with what is happening on the Black Continent, Africa. Look at the artifacts being discovered there, that are proving over and over again, how the black man had great, fine, sensitive civilizations before the white man was out of the caves. Below the Sahara, in the places where most of America's Negroes' foreparents were kidnapped, there is being unearthed some of the finest craftsmanship, sculpture and other objects, that has ever been seen by modern man. Some of these things now are on view in such places as New York City's Museum of Modern Art. Gold work of such fine tolerance and workmanship that it has no rival. Ancient objects produced by black hands . . . refined by those black hands with results that no human hand today can equal.

History has been so "whitened" by the white man that even the black professors have known little more than the most

---

* *The Autobiography of Malcolm X*, pp. 175-178.

ignorant black man about the talents and rich civilizations and cultures of the black man of millenniums ago. I have lectured in Negro colleges and some of these brainwashed black Ph. D.'s, with their suspenders dragging the ground with degrees, have run to the white man's newspapers calling me a "black fanatic." Why, a lot of them are fifty years behind the times. If I were president of one of these black colleges, I'd hock the campus if I had to, to send a bunch of black students off digging in Africa for more, more and more proof of the black race's historical greatness. The white man now is in Africa digging and searching. An African elephant can't stumble without falling on some white man with a shovel. Practically every week, we read about some great new find from Africa's lost civilizations. All that's new is white science's attitude. The ancient civilizations of the black man have been buried on the Black Continent all the time.

Here is an example: a British anthropologist named Dr. Louis S. B. Leakey is displaying some fossil bones — a foot, part of a hand, some jaws, and skull fragments. On the basis of these, Dr. Leakey has said it's time to rewrite completely the history of man's origin.

This species of man lived 1,818,036 years before Christ. And these bones were found in Tanganyika. In the Black Continent.

It's a crime, the lie that has been told to generations of black men and white men both. Little innocent black children, born of parents who believed that their race had no history. Little black children seeing, before they could talk, that their parents considered themselves inferior. Innocent black children growing up, living out their lives, dying of old age — and all of their lives ashamed of being black. But the truth is pouring out of the bag now. . . .*

---

* *The Autobiography of Malcolm X*, pp. 181-183.

(Top) A drawing of Timbuktu by an eighteenth-century European traveler.
(Bottom) A Belgian artist's illustration of African agricultural products and methods of cultivation in 1603.

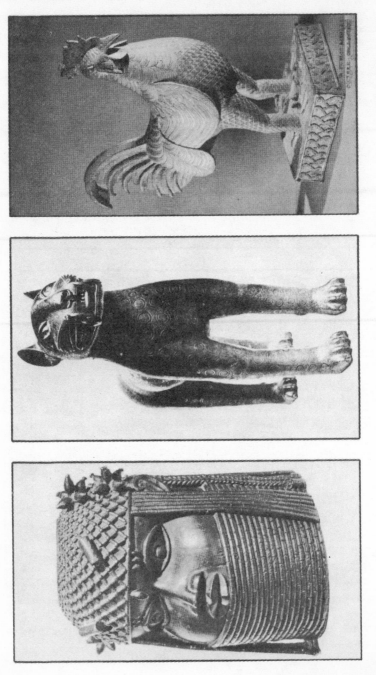

Benin bronzes: A man's head, a leopard, a rooster.

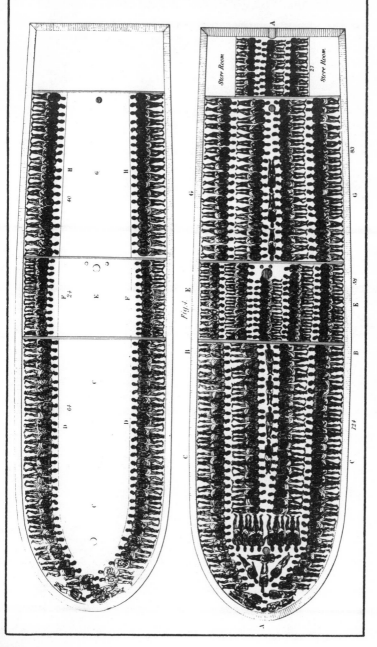

Loading diagram for two decks of a slave ship.

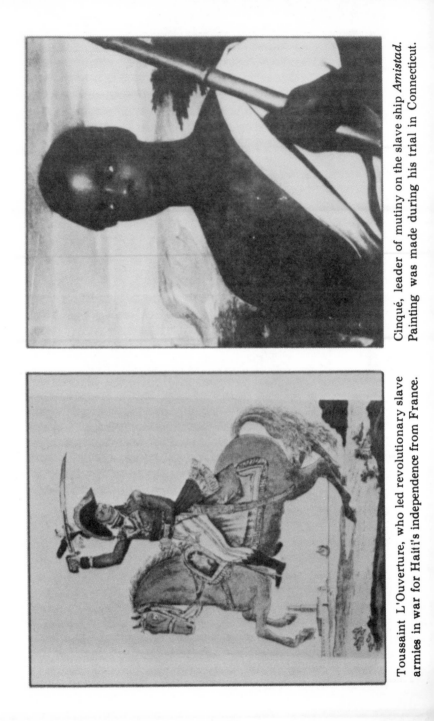

Cinqué, leader of mutiny on the slave ship *Amistad.* Painting was made during his trial in Connecticut.

Toussaint L'Ouverture, who led revolutionary slave armies in war for Haiti's independence from France.

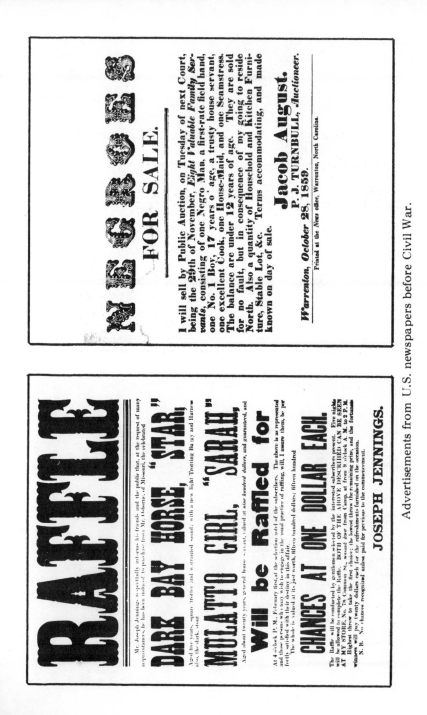

NEGROES

FOR SALE.

I will sell by Public Auction, on Tuesday of next Court, being the 29th of November, *Eight Valuable Family Servants*, consisting of one Negro Man, a first-rate field hand, one No. 1 Boy, 17 years o' age, a trusty house servant, one excellent Cook, one House-Maid, and one Seamstress. The balance are under 12 years of age. They are sold for no fault, but in consequence of my going to reside North. Also a quantity of Household and Kitchen Furniture, Stable Lot, &c. Terms accommodating, and made known on day of sale.

Jacob August.
P. J. TURNBULL, *Auctioneer.*

Warrenton, October 28, 1859.

Printed at the *News* office, Warrenton, North Carolina.

RAFFLE

Mr. Joseph Jennings respectfully informs his friends and the public that, at the request of many acquaintances, he has been induced to purchase-[*a*] that of Mr. Osborne, of Missouri, the celebrated

DARK BAY HORSE, "STAR,"

Aged five years, square trotter and warranted sound; with a new light Trotting Buggy and Harness also, the dark, stout

MULATTO GIRL, "SARAH,"

Aged about twenty years, general house servant, valued at *nine hundred dollars*, and guaranteed, and

Will be Raffled for

At 4 o'clock P. M. February first, at the selection noted of the subscribers. The above is as represented and those persons who may wish to engage in the usual practice of raffling, will, I assure them, be perfectly satisfied with their destiny in this affair.

The whole is valued at its just worth, fifteen hundred dollars; fifteen hundred

CHANCES AT ONE DOLLAR EACH.

The Raffle will be conducted by gentlemen selected by the interested subscribers present. Five nights will be allowed to complete the Raffle. BOTH OF THE ABOVE DESCRIBED CAN BE SEEN AT MY STORE, No. 78 Common St., several door from Camp, at from 9 o'clock A. M. to 2 P. M. Highest throw to take the first choice; the lowest throw the remaining prize, and the fortunate winners will pay twenty dollars each for the refreshments furnished on the occasion.

N. B. No chances recognized unless paid for previous to the commencement.

JOSEPH JENNINGS.

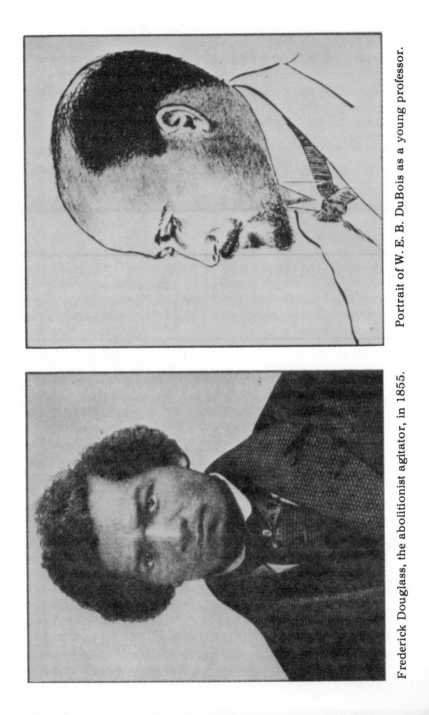

Frederick Douglass, the abolitionist agitator, in 1855.

Portrait of W. E. B. DuBois as a young professor.

Study History

Of all our studies, history is best qualified to reward our research. And when you see that you've got problems, all you have to do is examine the historic method used all over the world by others who have problems similar to yours. Once you see how they got theirs straight, then you know how you can get yours straight.

(Malcolm X Speaks, p. 8)

The House Negro and the Field Negro

Back during slavery, when people like me talked to the slaves, they didn't kill them, they sent some old house Negro along behind him to undo what he said. You have to read the history of slavery to understand this.

There were two kinds of Negroes. There was that old house Negro and the field Negro. And the house Negro always looked out for his master. When the field Negroes got too much out of line, he held them back in check. He put them back on the plantation.

The house Negro could afford to do that because he lived better than the field Negro. He ate better, he dressed better, and he lived in a better house. He lived right up next to his master — in the attic or in the basement. He ate the same food as his master and wore his same clothes. And he could talk just like his master — good diction. And he loved his master more than his master loved himself. That's why he didn't want his master to get hurt. If the master got sick, he'd say: "What's the matter, boss, we sick?"

When the master's house caught afire, he'd try and put out the fire. He didn't want his master's house burnt. He never wanted his master's property threatened. And he was more defensive of it than his master was. That was the house Negro.

But then you had some field Negroes, who lived in huts, had nothing to lose. They wore the worst kind of clothes. They ate the worst food. And they caught hell. They felt the sting of the lash. They hated this land.

You know what they did? If the master got sick, they'd

63

pray that the master'd die.

If the master's house caught afire, they'd pray for a strong wind to come along. This was the difference between the two.

And today you still have house Negroes and field Negroes.

I'm a field Negro. If I can't live in the house as a human being, I'm praying for a wind to come along. If the master won't treat me right and he's sick, I'll call the doctor to go in the other direction. But if all of us are going to live as human beings, then I'm for a society of human beings that can practice brotherhood.

(February 4, 1965)

The Missing 75 Million

One hundred million Africans were uprooted from the African continent—where are they today? One hundred million Africans were uprooted, 100 million Africans, according to the book, *Anti-Slavery*, by Professor Dwight Lowell Dumond—excuse me for raising my voice—were uprooted from the continent of Africa. At the end of slavery you didn't have 25 million Africans in the Western Hemisphere. What happened to those 75 million? Their bodies are at the bottom of the ocean, or their blood and their bones have fertilized the soil of this country.

(April 8, 1964)

Schoolbooks

(The quotation in the following passage is from a statement by the Organization of Afro-American Unity being read and commented on by Malcolm at the founding meeting of the OAAU:)

"The textbooks tell our children nothing about the great contribution of Afro-Americans to the growth and development of this country." And they don't. When we send our children to school in this country they learn nothing about us other than that we used to be cotton-pickers. Every little child going to school thinks his grandfather was a cotton-picker. Why, your grandfather was Nat Turner; your grandfather was Toussaint L'Ouverture; your grandfather was Hannibal. Your grandfather was some of the greatest black people who walked on this earth. It was your grandfather's hands who forged civilization and it was your grandmother's hands who rocked the cradle of civilization. But the textbooks tell our children nothing about the great contributions of Afro-Americans to the growth and development of this country.

(June 28, 1964)

A Poor Comparison

(On being told that old-age pensioners and black people have common interests:)

I don't see how you can compare their situation with the plight of 22 million African-Americans. Our people were outright slaves — outright slaves. We pulled plows like horses. We were bought and sold from one plantation to another like you sell chickens or like you sell a bag of potatoes. I read in one book where George Washington exchanged a black man for a bag of molasses. Why, that black man could have been my grandfather. You know what I think of old George Washington. You can't compare someone on old-age assistance with the plight of black people in this country. No comparison whatsoever. And what they can do is not comparable to what we can do — not those old folks.

(April 8, 1964)

The Mayflower

So we're all black people, so-called Negroes, second-class citizens, ex-slaves. You're nothing but an ex-slave. You don't like to be told that. But what else are you? You are ex-slaves. You didn't come here on the "Mayflower." You came here on a slave ship. In chains, like a horse, or a cow, or a chicken. And you were brought here by the people who came here on the "Mayflower," you were brought here by the so-called Pilgrims, or Founding Fathers. They were the ones who brought you here.

(Malcolm X Speaks, pp 4-5)

What Kind of Allies?

We need allies who are going to help us achieve a victory, not allies who are going to tell us to be nonviolent. If a white man wants to be an ally, ask him what does he think of John Brown. You know what John Brown did? He went to war. He was a white man who went to war against white people to help free slaves. He wasn't nonviolent. White people call John Brown a nut. Go read the history, go read what all of them say about John Brown. They're trying to make it look like he was a nut, a fanatic. They made a movie on it. I saw a movie on the screen one night. Why, I would be afraid to get near John Brown if I go by what other white folks say about him. But they depict him in this image because he was willing to shed blood to free the slaves. And any white man who is ready and willing to shed blood for your freedom — in the sight of other whites, he's nuts. As long as he wants to come up with some nonviolent action, they go for that. If he's a liberal, a nonviolent liberal, they love everybody liberal. But when it comes time for making the same kind of contribution for your and my freedom that was necessary for them to make for their own freedom they back out of the situation. So when you want to know good white folks in history where black people are concerned, go read the history of John Brown. That was what I call a white liberal. But those other kind, they are questionable. So if we need white allies in this country, we don't need those kind who compromise. We don't need those kind who encourage us to be polite, responsible, you know. We don't need those kind who give us that kind of advice. We don't need those kind who tell us how to be patient. No, if we need some white allies, we need the kind that John Brown was or we don't need you. And the only way to get those kind is to turn in a new direction.

(July 5, 1964)

Our Investment

You take the people who are in this audience right now. They're poor, we're all poor as individuals. Our weekly salary individually amounts to hardly anything. But if you take the salary of everyone in here collectively it'll fill up a whole lot of baskets. It's a lot of wealth. If you can collect the wages of just these people right here for a year, you'll be rich — richer than rich. When you look at it like that, think how rich Uncle Sam had to become, not with this handful, but millions of black people. Your and my mother and father, who didn't work an eight-hour shift, but worked from "can't see" in the morning until "can't see" at night, and worked for nothing, making the white man rich, making Uncle Sam rich.

This is our investment. This is our contribution — our blood. Not only did we give of our free labor, we gave of our blood. Every time he had a call to arms, we were the first ones in uniform. We died on every battlefield the white man had. We have made a greater sacrifice than anybody who's standing up in America today. We have made a greater contribution and have collected less. Civil rights, for those of us whose philosophy is black nationalism, means: "Give it to us now. Don't wait for next year. Give it to us yesterday, and that's not fast enough."

(*Malcolm X Speaks*, pp. 32-33)

Pay Up!

You've always had someone else to do your fighting for you. You perhaps haven't realized it. England became powerful because she had others to fight for her. She used the African against the Asian and the Asian against the African. France used the Senegalese. All these white powers have had some little lackeys to do their fighting for them, and America has had 22 million African-Americans to do your fighting for you. It was we who have fought your battles for you, and have picked your cotton for you. We built this house that you're living in. It was our labor that built this house. You sat beneath the old cotton tree telling us how long to work or how hard to work, but it was our labor, our sweat and our blood that made this country what it is, and we're the only ones who haven't benefited from it. All we're saying today is, it's payday — retroactive.

(April 8, 1964)

Selecting Heroes

(On being asked if he did not think it important for the new black generation to know about the slave revolts in America and people like Sojourner Truth and Frederick Douglass:)

Malcolm: Yes, it's important, but it's even more important for us to be re-established and connected to our roots. Douglass was great. I would rather have been taught about Toussaint L'Ouverture. We need to be taught about people who fought, who bled for freedom and made others bleed.

Questioner: The first guy that was shot at the moment of the War of Independence was a Negro.

Malcolm: He wasn't shot for Negroes. He was shot for America. I don't want to take away from Crispus Attucks, but he was shot. He was a slave. His people were slaves.

Questioner: He was a slave perhaps, but not on his knees — on his feet.

Malcolm: Sir, you can take a dog — a big vicious dog — and sic him on somebody else and he's fearless. I'd like to give you an example. No matter how fearless a dog is, you catch him out on the street, stomp your foot — he'll run because you're only threatening him. His master has never trained him how to defend himself, but that same dog — if you walk through the master's gate — will growl and bite. Why will he growl and bite over here and not growl and bite over here? Over here he's growling and biting for the defense of his master and the benefit of his master, but when his own interests are threatened he has no growl.

Not only Crispus Attucks, but many of us in America have died defending America. We defend our master. We're the most violent soldiers America has when she sends us to Korea or to the South Pacific or to Saigon, but when our mothers and our own property are being attacked we're nonviolent. Crispus Attucks laid down his life for America, but would he have laid down his life to stop the white man in America from enslaving black people?

So when you select heroes about which black people ought to be taught, let them be black heroes who have died fighting for the benefit of black people. We never were taught about Christophe or Dessalines. It was the slave revolt in Haiti when slaves, black slaves, had the soldiers of Napoleon tied down and forced him to sell one-half of the American continent to the Americans. They don't teach us that. That is the kind of history we want to learn.

(November 23, 1964)

The International Power Structure

I might point out here that colonialism or imperialism, as the slave system of the West is called, is not something that is just confined to England or France or the United States. The interests in this country are in cahoots with the interests in France and the interests in Britain. It's one huge complex or combine, and it creates what's known not as the American power structure or the French power structure, but an international power structure. This international power structure is used to suppress the masses of dark-skinned people all over the world and exploit them of their natural resources, so that the era in which you and I have been living during the past ten years most specifically has witnessed the upsurge on the part of the black man in Africa against the power structure.

He wants his freedom, and now. Mind you, the power structure is international, and its domestic base is in London, in Paris, in Washington, D. C., and so forth. The outside or external phase of the revolution which is manifest in the attitude and action of the Africans today is troublesome enough. The revolution on the outside of the house, or the outside of the structure, is troublesome enough. But now the powers that be are beginning to see that this struggle on the outside by the black man is affecting, infecting the black man who is on the inside of that structure — I hope you understand what I am trying to say. The newly awakened people all over the world pose a problem for what is known as Western interests, which is imperialism, colonialism, racism and all these other negative isms or vulturistic isms. Just as the external forces pose a grave threat, they can now see that the internal forces pose an even greater threat. But the internal forces pose an even greater threat only when they have properly analyzed the situation and know what the stakes really are.

(Malcolm X Speaks, pp. 168-169)

Periods of Advancement

Prior to 1939, our people were in a very menial position or condition. Most of us were waiters and porters and bellhops and janitors and waitresses and things of that sort. It was not until war was declared with Germany, and America became involved in a manpower shortage in regards to her factories plus her army, that the black man in this country was permitted to make a few strides forward. It was never out of some kind of moral enlightenment or moral awareness on the part of Uncle Sam. Uncle Sam only let the black man take a step forward when he himself had his back to the wall.

In Michigan, where I was brought up at that time, I recall that the best jobs in the city for blacks were waiters out at the country club. In those days if you had a job waiting table in the country club, you had it made. Or if you had a job at the State House. Having a job at the State House didn't mean that you were a clerk or something of that sort; you had a shoeshine stand at the State House. Just by being there you could be around all those big-shot politicians — that made you a big-shot Negro. You were shining shoes, but you were a big-shot Negro because you were around big-shot white people and you could bend their ear and get up next to them. And ofttimes you were chosen by them to be the voice of the Negro community.

Around that time, 1939 or '40 or '41, they weren't drafting Negroes in the army or the navy. A Negro couldn't join the navy in 1940 or '41. They wouldn't take a black man in the navy except to make him a cook. He couldn't just go and join the navy, and I don't think he could just go and join the army. They weren't drafting him when the war first started. This is what they thought of you and me in those days. For one thing, they didn't trust us; they feared that if they put us in the army and trained us in how to use rifles and other things, we might shoot at some targets that they hadn't picked out. And we would have. Any thinking man knows what target to shoot at. If a man has to have someone else to choose his target, then he isn't thinking for himself — they're doing the thinking for him.

The Negro leaders in those days were the same type we have today. When the Negro leaders saw all the white fellows being drafted and taken into the army and dying on the battlefield, and no Negroes were dying because they weren't being drafted, the Negro leaders came up and said, "We've got to die too. We want to be drafted too, and we demand that you take us in and let us die for our country too" . . . .

So they started drafting Negro soldiers then, and started letting Negroes get into the navy. But not until Hitler and Tojo and the foreign powers were strong enough to put pressure on this country, so that it had its back to the wall and needed us, [did] they let us work in factories. Up until that time we couldn't work in the factories; I'm talking about the North as well as the South. And when they let us work in the factories, at first they let us in only as janitors. After a year or so passed by, they let us work on machines. We became machinists, got a little more skill. If we got a little more skill, we made a little more money, which enabled us to live in a little better neighborhood. When we lived in a little better neighborhood, we went to a little better school, got a little better education and could come out and get a little better job. So the cycle was broken somewhat.

But the cycle was not broken out of some kind of sense of moral responsibility on the part of the government. No, the only time that cycle was broken even to a degree was when world pressure was brought to bear on the United States government. They didn't look at us as human beings — they just put us into their system and let us advance a little bit farther because it served their interests. . .

(Malcolm X Speaks, pp. 147-150)

Lessons of 1964

In 1964, oppressed people all over the world, in Africa, in Asia and Latin America, in the Caribbean, made some progress. Northern Rhodesia threw off the yoke of colonialism and became Zambia, and was accepted into the United Nations, the society of independent governments. Nyasaland became Malawi and also was accepted into the UN, into the family of independent governments. Zanzibar had a revolution, threw out the colonialists and their lackeys and then united with Tanganyika into what is now known as the Republic of Tanzania — which is progress, indeed. . . .

Also in 1964, the oppressed people of South Vietnam, and in that entire Southeast Asia area, were successful in fighting off the agents of imperialism. All the king's horses and all the king's men haven't enabled them to put North and South Vietnam together again. Little rice farmers, peasants, with a rifle — up against all the highly-mechanized weapons of warfare — jets, napalm, battleships, everything else, and they can't put those rice farmers back where they want them. Somebody's waking up.

In the Congo, the People's Republic of the Congo, headquartered at Stanleyville, fought a war for freedom against Tshombe, who is an agent for Western imperialism — and by Western imperialism I mean that which is headquartered in the United States, in the State Department.

In 1964 this government, subsidizing Tshombe, the murderer of Lumumba, and Tshombe's mercenaries, hired killers from South Africa, along with the former colonial power, Belgium, dropped paratroopers on the people of the Congo, used Cubans, that they had trained, to drop bombs on the people of the Congo with American-made planes — to no avail. The struggle is still going on, and America's man, Tshombe, is still losing.

All of this in 1964. Now, in speaking like this, it doesn't mean that I am anti-American. I am not. I'm not anti-American, or un-American. And I'm not saying that to defend myself. Because if I was that, I'd have a right to be that — after what America has done to us. This government should feel lucky that our people aren't anti-American. They should get down on their hands and knees every morning and thank God that 22 million black people have not become anti-American. You've given us every right to. The whole world would side with us, if we became anti-American. You know, that's something to think about.

But we are not anti-American. We are anti or against what America is doing wrong in other parts of the world as well as here. And what she did in the Congo in 1964 is wrong. It's criminal, criminal. And what she did to the American public, to get the American public to go along with it, is criminal. What she's doing in South Vietnam is criminal. She's causing American soldiers to be murdered every day, killed every day, die every day, for no reason at all. That's wrong. Now, you're not supposed to be so blind with patriotism that you can't face reality. Wrong is wrong, no matter who does it or who says it. . . .

(*Malcolm X Speaks*, pp. 156-158)

Africa and Self-Hate

Now what effect does [the struggle over Africa] have on us? Why should the black man in America concern himself since he's been away from the African continent for three or four hundred years? Why should we concern ourselves? What impact does what happens to them have upon us? Number one, you have to realize that up until 1959 Africa was dominated by the colonial powers. Having complete control over Africa, the colonial powers of Europe projected the image of Africa negatively. They always project Africa in a negative light: jungle savages, cannibals, nothing civilized. Why then naturally it was so negative that it was negative to you and me, and you and I began to hate it. We didn't want anybody telling us anything about Africa, much less calling us Africans. In hating Africa and in hating the Africans, we ended up hating ourselves, without even realizing it. Because you can't hate the roots of a tree, and not hate the tree. You can't hate your origin and not end up hating yourself. You can't hate Africa and not hate yourself.

You show me one of these people over here who has been thoroughly brainwashed and has a negative attitude toward Africa, and I'll show you one who has a negative attitude toward himself. You can't have a positive attitude toward yourself and a negative attitude toward Africa at the same

73

time. To the same degree that your understanding of and attitude toward Africa become positive, you'll find that your understanding of and your attitude toward yourself will also become positive. And this is what the white man knows. So they very skilfully make you and me hate our African identity, our African characteristics.

You know yourself that we have been a people who hated our African characteristics. We hated our heads, we hated the shape of our nose, we wanted one of those long dog-like noses, you know; we hated the color of our skin, hated the blood of Africa that was in our veins. And in hating our features and our skin and our blood, why, we had to end up hating ourselves. And we hated ourselves. Our color became to us a chain—we felt that it was holding us back; our color became to us like a prison which we felt was keeping us confined, not letting us go this way or that way. We felt that all of these restrictions were based solely upon our color, and the psychological reaction to that would have to be that as long as we felt imprisoned or chained or trapped by black skin, black features and black blood, that skin and those features and that blood holding us back automatically had to become hateful to us. And it became hateful to us.

It made us feel inferior; it made us feel inadequate; made us feel helpless. And when we fell victims to this feeling of inadequacy or inferiority or helplessness, we turned to somebody else to show us the way. We didn't have confidence in another black man to show us the way, or black people to show us the way. In those days we didn't. We didn't think a black man could do anything except play some horns—you know, make some sound and make you happy with some songs and in that way. But in serious things, where our food, clothing, shelter and education were concerned, we turned to the man. We never thought in terms of bringing these things into existence for ourselves, we never thought in terms of doing things for ourselves. Because we felt helpless. What made us feel helpless was our hatred for ourselves. And our hatred for ourselves stemmed from our hatred for things African. . . .

(*Malcolm X Speaks*, pp. 184-185)